Whole Language Approach

Internet-Aided English Learning 1

SELECTED TOP

Epoch-Making Speeches

Abraham LINCOLN • John F. KENNEDY.
Winston CHURCHILL • Margaret THATCHER.
Barak OBAMA • Bill GATES
Ben FRANKLIN • Steve JOBS.
Martin Luther KING, Jr. • Tony BLAIR
Babe RUTH • Frank ROOSEVELT

이 봉 형 지음
영어감수 Bryn Elizabeth Keating

Shinasa

SELECTED TOP

Epoch Making Speeches

CONTENTS

Preface

In the current global era, it is quite a demanding job to teach and learn English. Enhancing one's foreign language skills to the level of native speakers comes to be Jack and Jill's ardent aspiration in our society. For the instructors and learners alike who have had no sufficient experiences to immerse in the ocean of English, it is not such a happy situation.

As with English or other foreign languages, Korean society moves abruptly from reading–focused learning to speaking–focused orientation. In light of the nature of language, the trend of speaking–first itself is not to blame. Yet, the thing is that every man engaged in ESL tasks is not well–prepared enough to handle the wanton demands and expectations.

As one of those who have commonly felt embarrassed by and uncomfortable with this common situation, I wanted to develop a type of teaching material to tide over this frightening setting looming over us. Most of the address articles in this collection are selected from epoch–making addresses delivered by historic figures in modern history.

The articles were found serendipitously when I surfed the Internet. I was lucky to bump into websites displaying renowned speeches delivered by terrific celebrities. One major source is *American Rhetoric: Online Speech Bank* (URL: www.americanrhetoric.com). The content of the speeches may already be familiar to you. However, regardless of your degree of familiarity, they will surely be useful in building up and raising your English skills.

To relieve monotony and boredom for students in the class, I tried to find as many video materials as possible from the websites. Unfortunately, however, many of the speeches were written when video footage was not widely available, for instance, Benjamin Franklin's *On the Constitution* (1787); and Abraham Lincoln's *Gettysburg Address* (1863). In that case, I had to present only the audio versions along with the scripts or, in the worst cases, just texts are provided.

For the definitions for words and expressions, we substantially rely upon an Internet dictionary whose address is dictionary.reference.com For the sake of simplicity, further acknowledgement will not be attempted in the body of this book.

Last but not least, I tried to include addresses stemming from both American and British English territories. This effort aims to embrace my intention for the students to pick up on American and British dialects at once, whatever media we go through. I hope this collection is very helpful to all prospective users.

Epoch-Making Speeches

General Directions:

Before you read the scripts, be sure to listen to the audio or go through the video versions first. Remember we are aiming to get used to and eventually pick up the style, and expressions appearing in the speeches, aside from their content.

Be sure to listen to the speeches at least twice before you read the transcripts.

Before starting to listen, be sure to scan the Exercises, which foreshadow the content or expressions in the text, in advance. Make sure that you can answer the given questions and problems properly after the completion of listening or reading. Please put forth your answers in your own way. Get away from someone else' style of descriptions. Remember that some of questions are open-ended.

Audio or video versions of the speeches will be available on the Internet. One huge website that makes the great speeches available is www.americanrhetoric.com. Go to the sites and download the video or audio materials onto your USB or MP3 player or other electronic storage devices.

Listening and writing components will be solicited to be included as test items in mid-term and final tests.

1 Epoch-Making Speeches

Inauguration Address

delivered on January 20, 2009

by **Barak Obama**

http://www.youtube.com/watch?v=VjnygQ02aW4

Chief Justice, Supreme Court : Are you prepared to take the oath, Senator?

Obama : I am.

Chief Justice : I, Barak Hussein Obama do solemnly swear that I will execute the office of president to the United States faithfully; (repeated by Barak Obama).

And will, to the best of my ability to preserve, protect and defend the constitution of the United States. (repeated by Barak Obama)

So help you God! Congratulations, Mr. President!

Public announcement : It's my great pursuit of honor to present the 44th President of these United States, Barak Obama.

* * * * * *

My fellow citizens: I stand here today humbled by the task before us, grateful for the trust you've bestowed, mindful of the sacrifices borne by our ancestors.

I thank President Bush for his service to our nation — *(applause)* — as well as the generosity and cooperation he has shown throughout this transition.

Forty-four Americans have now taken the presidential oath. The words have been spoken during rising tides of prosperity and the still waters of peace. Yet, every so often, the oath is taken amidst gathering clouds and raging storms. At these moments, America has carried on not simply because of the skill or vision of those in high office, but because we, the people, have remained faithful to the ideals of our forebears and true to our founding documents.

So it has been; so it must be with this generation of Americans.

That we are in the midst of crisis is now well understood. Our nation is at war against a far-reaching network of violence and hatred. Our economy is badly weakened, a consequence of greed and irresponsibility on the part of some, but also our collective failure to make hard choices and prepare the nation for a new age. Homes have been lost, jobs shed, businesses shuttered. Our health care is too costly, our schools fail too many — and each day brings further evidence that the ways we use energy strengthen our adversaries and threaten our planet.

These are the indicators of crisis, subject to data and statistics. Less measurable, but no less profound, is a sapping of confidence across our land; a nagging fear that America's decline is inevitable, that the next generation must lower its sights.

Today I say to you that the challenges we face are real. They are serious and they are many. They will not be met easily or in a short span of time. But know this America: They will be met. (Applause.)

On this day, we gather because we have chosen hope over fear, unity of purpose over conflict and discord. On this day, we come to proclaim an end to the petty grievances and false promises, the recriminations and worn-out dogmas that for far too long have strangled our politics. We remain a young nation. But in the words of Scripture, the time has come to set aside childish things. The time has come to reaffirm our enduring spirit; to choose our better history; to carry forward that precious gift, that noble idea passed on from generation to generation: the God-given promise that all are equal, all are free, and all deserve a chance to pursue their full measure of happiness. (Applause.)

In reaffirming the greatness of our nation we understand that greatness is never a given. It must be earned. Our journey has never been one of short-cuts or settling for less. It has not been the path for the faint-hearted, for those that prefer leisure over work, or seek only the pleasures of riches and fame. Rather, it has been the risk-takers, the doers, the makers of things — some celebrated, but more often men and women obscure in their labor — who have carried us up the long rugged path towards prosperity and freedom.

For us, they packed up their few worldly possessions and traveled across oceans in search of a new life. For us, they toiled in sweatshops, and settled the West, endured the lash of the whip, and plowed the hard earth. For us, they fought and died in places like Concord and Gettysburg, Normandy and Khe Sahn.

Time and again these men and women struggled and sacrificed and worked till their hands were raw so that we might live a better life. They saw America as bigger than the sum of our individual ambitions, greater than all the differences of birth or wealth or faction.

This is the journey we continue today. We remain the most prosperous, powerful nation on Earth. Our workers are no less productive than when this crisis began. Our minds are no less inventive, our goods and services no less needed than they were last week, or last month, or last year. Our capacity remains undiminished. But our time of standing pat, of protecting narrow interests and putting off unpleasant decisions — that time has surely passed. Starting today, we must pick ourselves up, dust ourselves off, and begin again the work of remaking America. (Applause.)

For everywhere we look, there is work to be done. The state of our economy calls for action, bold and swift. And we will act, not only to create new jobs, but to lay a new foundation for growth. We will build the roads and bridges, the electric grids and digital lines that feed our commerce and bind us together. We'll restore science to its rightful place, and wield technology's wonders to raise health care's quality and lower its cost. We will harness the sun and the winds and the soil to fuel our cars and run our factories. And we will transform our schools and colleges and universities to meet the demands of a new age. All this we can do. All this we will do.

Now, there are some who question the scale of our ambitions, who suggest that our system cannot tolerate too many big plans. Their memories are short, for they have forgotten what this country has already done, what free men and women can achieve when imagination is joined to common purpose, and necessity to courage. What the cynics fail to understand is that the ground has shifted beneath them, that the stale political arguments that have consumed us for so long no longer apply.

The question we ask today is not whether our government is too big or too small, but whether it works — whether it helps families find jobs at a decent wage, care they can afford, a retirement that is dignified. Where the answer is yes, we intend to move forward. Where the answer is no, programs will end. And those of us who manage the public's dollars will be held to account, to spend wisely, reform bad habits, and do our business in the light of day, because only then can we restore the vital trust between a people and their government.

Nor is the question before us whether the market is a force for good or ill. Its power to generate wealth and expand freedom is unmatched. But this crisis has reminded us that without a watchful eye, the market can spin out of control. The nation cannot prosper long when it favors only the prosperous. The success of our economy has always depended not just on the size of our gross domestic product, but on the reach of our prosperity, on the ability to extend opportunity to every willing heart — not out of charity, but because it is the surest route to our common good. (Applause.)

As for our common defense, we reject as false the choice between our safety and our ideals. Our Founding Fathers — (applause) — our Founding Fathers, faced with perils that we can scarcely imagine, drafted a charter to assure the rule of law and the rights of man — a charter expanded by the blood of generations. Those ideals still light the world, and we will not give them up for expedience sake. (Applause.)

And so, to all the other peoples and governments who are watching today, from the grandest capitals to the small village where my father was born, know that America is a friend of each nation, and every man, woman and child who seeks a future of peace and dignity. And we are ready to lead once more. (Applause.)

Recall that earlier generations faced down fascism and communism not just with missiles and tanks, but with the sturdy alliances and enduring convictions. They understood that our power alone cannot protect us, nor does it entitle us to do as we please. Instead they knew that our power grows through its prudent use; our security emanates from the justness of our cause, the force of our example, the tempering qualities of humility and restraint.

We are the keepers of this legacy. Guided by these principles once more we can meet those new threats that demand even greater effort, even greater cooperation and understanding between nations. We will begin to responsibly leave Iraq to its people and forge a hard-earned peace in Afghanistan. With old friends and former foes, we'll work tirelessly to lessen the nuclear threat, and roll back the specter of a warming planet.

We will not apologize for our way of life, nor will we waver in its defense. And for those who seek to advance their aims by inducing terror and slaughtering innocents, we say to you now that our spirit is stronger and cannot be broken — you cannot outlast us, and we will defeat you. (Applause.)

For we know that our patchwork heritage is a strength, not a weakness. We are a nation of Christians and Muslims, Jews and Hindus, and non-believers. We are shaped by every language and culture, drawn from every end of this Earth; and because we have tasted the bitter swill of civil war and segregation, and emerged from that dark chapter stronger and more united, we cannot help but believe that the old hatreds shall someday pass; that the lines of tribe shall soon dissolve; that as the world grows smaller, our common humanity shall reveal itself; and that America must play its role in ushering in a new era of peace.

To the Muslim world, we seek a new way forward, based on mutual interest and mutual respect. To those leaders around the globe who seek to sow conflict, or blame their society's ills on the West, know that your people will judge you on what you can build, not what you destroy. (Applause.)

To those who cling to power through corruption and deceit and the silencing of dissent, know that you are on the wrong side of history, but that we will extend a hand if you are willing to unclench your fist. (Applause.)

To the people of poor nations, we pledge to work alongside you to make your farms flourish and let clean waters flow; to nourish starved bodies and feed hungry minds. And to those nations like ours that enjoy relative plenty, we say we can no longer afford indifference to the suffering outside our borders, nor can we consume the world's resources without regard to effect. For the world has changed, and we must change with it.

As we consider the role that unfolds before us, we remember with humble gratitude those brave Americans who at this very hour patrol far-off deserts and distant mountains. They have something to tell us, just as the fallen heroes who lie in Arlington whisper through the ages.

We honor them not only because they are the guardians of our liberty, but because they embody the spirit of service — a willingness to find meaning in something greater than themselves.

And yet at this moment, a moment that will define a generation, it is precisely this spirit that must inhabit us all. For as much as government can do, and must do, it is ultimately the faith and determination of the American people upon which this nation relies. It is the kindness to take in a stranger when the levees break, the selflessness of workers who would rather cut their hours than see a friend lose their job which sees us through our darkest hours. It is the firefighter's courage to storm a stairway filled with smoke, but also a parent's willingness to nurture a child that finally decides our fate.

Our challenges may be new. The instruments with which we meet them may be new. But those values upon which our success depends — honesty and hard work, courage and fair play, tolerance and curiosity, loyalty and patriotism — these things are old. These things are true. They have been the quiet force of progress throughout our history.

What is demanded, then, is a return to these truths. What is required of us now is a new era of responsibility — a recognition on the part of every American that we have duties to ourselves, our nation and the world; duties that we do not grudgingly accept, but rather seize gladly, firm in the knowledge that there is nothing so satisfying to the spirit, so defining of our character than giving our all to a difficult task.

This is the price and the promise of citizenship. This is the source of our confidence — the knowledge that God calls on us to shape an uncertain destiny. This is the meaning of our liberty and our creed, why men and women and children of every race and every faith can join in celebration across this magnificent mall; and why a man whose father less than 60 years ago might not have been served in a local restaurant can now stand before you to take a most sacred oath. (Applause.)

So let us mark this day with remembrance of who we are and how far we have traveled. In the year of America's birth, in the coldest of months, a small band of patriots huddled by dying campfires on the shores of an icy river. The capital was abandoned. The enemy was advancing. The snow was stained with blood. At the moment when the outcome of our revolution was most in doubt, the father of our nation ordered these words to be read to the people:

"Let it be told to the future world...that in the depth of winter, when nothing but hope and virtue could survive... that the city and the country, alarmed at one common danger, came forth to meet [it]."

America: In the face of our common dangers, in this winter of our hardship, let us remember these timeless words. With hope and virtue, let us brave once more the icy currents, and endure what storms may come. Let it be said by our children's children that when we were tested we refused to let this journey end, that we did not turn back nor did we falter; and with eyes fixed on the horizon and God's grace upon us, we carried forth that great gift of freedom and delivered it safely to future generations.

Thank you. God bless you. And God bless the United States of America. (Applause.)

Words and Expressions Check-Up

humble *verb* to lower in condition or dignity.

transition *noun* change from one position or state, stage to another.

carry on *phrasal verb* to continue without stopping: *Rescue operations were carried on in spite of the torrential rainfalls.*

forebear *noun* ancestors, forefathers.

far-reaching *adjective* extending far in influence or effect: *the far-reaching effect of his appointment.*

shed *verb* to cast off or let fall leaves, hair, shell, etc. by natural process.

sap *verb* to undermine, weaken or destroy secretly.

recriminate *verb* to accuse in return.

strangle *verb* to kill by stopping the breath, choke, suffocate.

sweatshop *noun* a shop employing workers at low wages, and under poor conditions.

stand pat *idiom* to cling or hold firm to one's decision or beliefs: *The prime minister must stand pat in its policy.*

electric grid *noun* electric power transmission, a process in the delivery of electricity to consumers.

harness *verb* to bring under conditions for effective use: *to harness wind power.*

stale *adjective* having lost novelty or interest, hackneyed: *a stale pizza.*

unmatched *adjective* without equal or rival.

temper *verb* to soften or tone down, to bring to a proper, suitable, or desirable state by blending or admixture.

spectre *noun* some object or source of terror or dread.

waver *verb* to sway to and fro; flutter: *The foliage constantly wavers in the breeze.*

forge *verb* to form or make by concentrated effort.

patchwork *noun* something made up of an incongruous variety of pieces or parts, hodgepodge: *a patchwork of ideas.*

swill *noun* liquid or partly liquid food for animals, especially kitchen refuse given to swine.

unclench *verb* to open or become opened from a clenched state.

✓**Arlington** The battles of Lexington and Concord

were the first military engagements of the American Revolutionary War. They were fought on April 19, 1775, in Middlesex County, Province of Massachusetts Bay, within the towns of Lexington, Concord, Lincoln, Menotomy(present-day Arlington), and Cambridge, near Boston. The battles marked the outbreak of open armed conflict between the Kingdom of Great Britain and its thirteen colonies in the mainland of British North America. (The text and image are from www.wikipedia.org)

✓**Gettysburg Campaign** The Gettysburg Campaign was a series of battles fought in June and July 1863, during the American Civil War. After his victory in the Battle of Chancellorsville, Confederate General Robert E. Lee's Army of Northern Virginia moved north for offensive operations in Maryland and Pennsylvania. The Union Army of the Potomac, commanded by Maj. Gen. Joseph Hooker and Maj. Gen. George G. Meade(from June 28), pursued Lee, defeated him at the Battle of Gettysburg, but allowed him to escape back to Virginia.

The Battle of Khe Sanh (Operation Scotland and Operation Pegasus) It was conducted in northwestern Quang Tri Province, Republic of Vietnam (South Vietnam), between 21 January and 8 April 1968 during the Vietnam War. The combatants were elements of the United States (U.S.) III Marine Amphibious Force (III MAF), elements of the South Vietnamese Army of the Republic of Vietnam (ARVN) and two to three division-size elements of the People's Army of Vietnam (PAVN). The American command in South Vietnam gave the defense of the base the nickname Operation Scotland. (The text and image are from www.wikipeida.com)

levee *noun* an embankment designed to prevent the flooding of a river.

huddle *verb* to crouch or draw oneself together.

timeless *adjective* without beginning or end, eternal, everlasting.

brave *verb* to meet or face courageously: *to brave a danger.*

falter *verb* to hesitate or waver in action or intent: *Her courage did not falter at the hardship.*

Unscramble the words to complete a sentence.

the soccer/ because/ canceled/ of raging/ match/ storms/ was in the midst of/ this nation/ confusion/ is

seek/ riches/ and/ the youngsters/ only/ fame

a liar/ whether/ is / the question/ he is/or not

the/ crazy/ is/ out of/ control/ man

it is / give up / sake of / the plan / unwise / to / for / expedience

not/ served/ black/ theatre/ people/ were/ in the

Complete a sentence by filling out the blanks.

시시한 불평불만은 도움이 안 된다.

________ ________ are not helpful.

성공은 주어지는 것이 아니라 얻는 것이다.

Success is not ______, but it is ________.

이 약은 심약한 사람에게 효과가 있다

This medicine is good for the ______-________.

이름 있는 사람, 이름 없는 사람 모두가 필요하다.

We need some _______ people as well as _________ ones.

일어나서 먼지를 털어라.

______ yourself _____, and ______ yourself ______.

지도자들은 언행을 조심할 책임이 있다.

Leaders are ________ to_______ to be cautions in their language and actions.

우리가 너희보다 오래 버틸 것이다.

We will ________ you.

마지못해서 그 제안을 수락하게 되었다.

We ________ accepted the offer.

천성 위에 교육이 있다.

________ is above nature.

Listen and Fill in the Blanks.

This is the journey we continue today. We _________ the most prosperous, powerful nation on Earth. Our workers are _____ ________ productive than when this crisis began. Our minds are no less _________, our goods and services no less ________ than they were last week, or last month, or last year. Our capacity remains undiminished. But our time of standing pat, of protecting narrow interests and ________ _______ unpleasant decisions —that time has surely passed. Starting today, we must _______ ______ _______, dust ourselves off, and begin again the work of remaking America. (Applause.)

For everywhere we look, _____ _____ ______ to be done. The state of our economy calls for action, bold and swift. And we will act, not only to create new _______, but to lay a new foundation for growth. We will build the roads and bridges, the ________ _______ and ________ _________ that feed our commerce and bind us together. We'll restore science to its rightful place, and _________ technology's wonders to raise health care's quality and lower its cost. We will ________ the sun and the winds and the soil to ________ our cars and run our factories. And we will transform our schools and colleges and universities to _________ the demands of a new age. All this we can do. All this we will do.

To Develop Critical Thinking

President Obama promised to resolve the economic meltdown of the US. In retrospect, do you think that he successfully coped with the adversity and normalized the US economy?

The Star-Spangled Banner

The "Star-Spangled Banner" is the national anthem of the United States of America. The lyrics come from "Defence of Fort McHenry", a poem written in 1814 by the 35-year-old amateur poet Francis Scott Key after witnessing the bombardment of Fort McHenry by Royal Navy ships in Chesapeake Bay during the Battle of Baltimore in the War of 1812.

The poem was set to the tune of a popular British drinking song, written by John Stafford Smith for the Anacreontic Society, a men's social club in London. "The Anacreontic Song" (or "To Anacreon in Heaven"), set to various lyrics, was already popular in the United States. Set to Key's poem and renamed "The Star-Spangled Banner", it would soon become a well-known American patriotic song. With a range of one and a half octaves, it is known for being difficult to sing. Although the song has four stanzas, only the first is commonly sung today, with the fourth ("O thus be it ever when free men shall stand...") added on more formal occasions.

"The Star-Spangled Banner" was recognized for official use by the Navy in 1889 and the President in 1916, and was made the national anthem by a congressional resolution on March 3, 1931 (46 Stat. 1508, codified at 36 U.S.C. § 301), which was signed by President Herbert Hoover.

Before 1931, other songs served as the hymns of American officialdom. "My Country, 'Tis of Thee", whose melody was derived from the British national anthem, served as a de facto national anthem of the United States before the adoption of "The Star-Spangled Banner"; and "Hail, Columbia," served as the de facto national anthem from Washington's time and through the 18th and 19th centuries. Following the War of 1812 and subsequent American wars, other songs would emerge to compete for popularity at public events, among them "The Star-Spangled Banner".

www.wikipedia.org

Stanford University Commencement Speech

delivered on June 12, 2005.

by **Steve Jobs**

http://www.youtube.com/watch?v=UF8uR6Z6KLc

'You've got to find what you love,' Steve Jobs says

I am honored to be with you today at your commencement from one of the finest universities in the world. Truth be told, I never graduated from college. This is the closest I've ever gotten to a college graduation. Today I want to tell you three stories from my life. That's it. No big deal. Just three stories.

The first story is about connecting the dots.

I dropped out of Reed College after the first 6 months, but then stayed around as a drop-in for another 18 months or so before I really quit. So why did I drop out?

Stanford University Hoover Tower
from www.wikipedia.org

It started before I was born. My biological mother was a young, unwed college graduate student, and she decided to put me up for adoption. She felt very strongly that I should be adopted by college graduates, so everything was all set for me to be adopted at birth by a lawyer and his wife. Except that when I popped out they decided at the last minute that they really wanted a girl. So my parents, who were on a waiting list, got a call in the middle of the night asking: "We've an unexpected baby boy; do you want him?" They said: "Of course." My biological mother later found out that my mother had never graduated from college and that my father had never graduated from high school. She refused to sign the final adoption papers. She only relented a few months later when my parents promised that I would go to college. This is the start in my life.

And 17 years later I did go to college. But I naively chose a college that was almost as expensive as Stanford, and all of my working-class parents' savings were being spent on my college tuition. After six months, I couldn't see the value in it. I had no idea what I wanted to do with my life and no idea how college was going to help me figure it out. And here I was spending all of the money my parents had saved their entire life. So I decided to drop out and trust that it would all work out OK. It was pretty scary at the time, but looking back it was one of the best decisions I ever made. The minute I dropped out I could stop taking the required classes that didn't interest me, and begin dropping in on the ones that looked interesting.

It wasn't all romantic. I didn't have a dorm room, so I slept on the floor in friends' rooms, I returned coke bottles for the 5¢ deposits to buy food with, and I would walk the 7 miles across town every Sunday night to get one good meal a week at the Hare Krishna temple. I loved it. And much of what I stumbled into by following my curiosity and intuition turned out to be priceless later on. Let me give you one example:

Reed College at that time offered perhaps the best calligraphy instruction in the country. Throughout the campus every poster, every label on every drawer, was beautifully hand calligraphed. Because I had dropped out and didn't have to take the normal classes, I decided to take a calligraphy class to learn how to do this. I learned about serif and san serif typefaces, about varying the amount of space between different letter combinations, about what makes great typography great. It was beautiful, historical, artistically subtle in a way that science can't capture, and I found it fascinating.

None of this had even a hope of any practical application in my life. But ten years later, when we were designing the first Macintosh computer, it all came back to me. And we designed it all into the Mac. It was the first computer with beautiful typography. If I had never dropped in on that single course in college, the Mac would have never had multiple typefaces or proportionally spaced fonts. And since Windows just copied the Mac, its likely that no personal computer would have them. If I had never dropped out, I would have never dropped in on this calligraphy class, and personal computers might not have the wonderful typography that they do. Of course it was impossible to connect the dots looking forward when I was in college. But it was very, very clear looking backwards ten years later.

Again, you can't connect the dots looking forward; you can only connect them looking backwards. So you have to trust that the dots will somehow connect in your future. You have to trust in something — your gut, destiny, life, karma, whatever. Because believing that the dots will connect down that road will give you the confidence to follow your heart, even when it leads you off the well-worn path, and that will make all the difference.

My second story is about love and loss.

I was lucky — I found what I loved to do early in life. Woz and I started Apple in my parents garage when I was 20. We worked hard, and in 10 years Apple had grown from just the two of us in a garage into a $2 billion company with over 4000 employees. We had just released our finest creation — the Macintosh — a year earlier, and I had just turned 30. And then I got fired. How can you get fired from a company you started? Well, as Apple grew we hired someone who I thought was very talented to run the company with me, and for the first year or so things went well. But then our visions of the future began to diverge and eventually we had a falling out. When we did, our Board of Directors sided with him. So at 30 I was out. And very publicly out. What had been the focus of my entire adult life was gone, and it was devastating.

I really didn't know what to do for a few months. I felt that I had let the previous generation of entrepreneurs down — that I had dropped the baton as it was being passed to me. I met with David Packard and Bob Noyce and tried to apologize for screwing up so badly. I was a very public failure, and I even thought about running away from the valley. But something slowly began to dawn on me — I still loved what I did. The turn of events at Apple had not changed that one bit. I had been rejected, but I was still in love. And so I decided to start over.

I didn't see it then, but it turned out that getting fired from Apple was the best thing that could have ever happened to me. The heaviness of being successful was replaced by the lightness of being a beginner again, less sure about everything. It freed me to enter one of the most creative periods of my life.

During the next five years, I started a company named NeXT, another company named Pixar, and fell in love with an amazing woman who would become my wife. Pixar went on to create the worlds first computer animated feature film, *Toy Story*, and is now the most successful animation studio in the world. In a remarkable turn of events, Apple bought NeXT, I returned to Apple, and the technology we developed at NeXT is at the heart of Apple's current renaissance. And Laurene and I have a wonderful family together.

I'm pretty sure none of this would have happened if I hadn't been fired from Apple. It was awful tasting medicine, but I guess the patient needed it. Sometimes life hits you in the head with a brick. Don't lose faith. I'm convinced that the only thing that kept me going was that I loved what I did. You've got to find what you love. And that is as true for your work as it is for your lovers. Your work is going to fill a large part of your life, and the only way to be truly satisfied is to do what you believe is great work. And the only way to do great work is to love what you do. If you haven't found it yet, keep looking. Don't settle. As with all matters of the heart, you'll know when you find it. And, like any great relationship, it just gets better and better as the years roll on. So keep looking until you find it. Don't settle.

My third story is about death.

When I was 17, I read a quote that went something like: "If you live each day as if it was your last, someday you'll most certainly be right." It made an impression on me, and since then, for the past 33 years, I have looked in the mirror every morning and asked myself: "If today were the last day of my life, would I want to do what I am about to do today?" And whenever the answer has been "No" for too many days in a row, I know I need to change something.

Remembering that I'll be dead soon is the most important tool I've ever encountered to help me make the big choices in life. Because almost everything — all external expectations, all pride, all fear of embarrassment or failure — these things just fall away in the face of death, leaving only what is truly important. Remembering that you are going to die is the best way I know to avoid the trap of thinking you have something to lose. You are already naked. There is no reason not to follow your heart.

About a year ago I was diagnosed with cancer. I had a scan at 7:30 in the morning, and it clearly showed a tumor on my pancreas. I didn't even know what a pancreas was. The doctors told me this was almost certainly a type of cancer that is incurable, and that I should expect to live no longer than three to six months. My doctor advised me to go home and get my affairs in order, which is doctor's code for prepare to die. It means to try to tell your kids everything you thought you'd have the next 10 years to tell them in just a few months. It means to make sure everything is buttoned up so that it will be as easy as possible for your family. It means to say your goodbyes.

I lived with that diagnosis all day. Later that evening I had a biopsy, where they stuck an endoscope down my throat, through my stomach and into my intestines, put a needle into my pancreas and got a few cells from the tumor. I was sedated, but my wife, who was there, told me that when they viewed the cells under a microscope the doctors started crying because it turned out to be a very rare form of pancreatic cancer that is curable with surgery. I had the surgery and thankfully I'm fine now.

This was the closest I've been to facing death, and I hope its the closest I get for a few more decades. Having lived through it, I can now say this to you with a bit more certainty than when death was a useful but purely intellectual concept:

No one wants to die. Even people who want to go to heaven don't want to die to get there. And yet death is the destination we all share. No one has ever escaped it. And that is as it should be, because Death is very likely the single best invention of Life. It is Life's change agent. It clears out the old to make way for the new. Right now the new is you, but someday not too long from now, you will gradually become the old and be cleared away. Sorry to be so dramatic, but it is quite true.

Your time is limited, so don't waste it living someone else's life. Don't be trapped by dogma — which is living with the results of other people's thinking. Don't let the noise of others' opinions drown out your own inner voice. And most important, have the courage to follow your heart and intuition. They somehow already know what you truly want to become. Everything else is secondary.

When I was young, there was an amazing publication called *The Whole Earth Catalog*, which was one of the bibles of my generation. It was created by a fellow named Stewart Brand not far from here in Menlo Park, and he brought it to life with his poetic touch. This was in the late 1960's, before personal computers and desktop publishing, so it was all made with typewriters, scissors, and polaroid cameras. It was sort of like Google in paperback form, 35 years before Google came along: it was idealistic, and overflowing with neat tools and great notions.

Stewart and his team put out several issues of *The Whole Earth Catalog*, and then when it had run its course, they put out a final issue. It was the mid-1970s, and I was your age. On the back cover of their final issue was a photograph of an early morning country road, the kind you might find yourself hitchhiking on if you were so adventurous. Beneath it were the words: "Stay Hungry. Stay Foolish." It was their farewell message as they signed off. Stay Hungry. Stay Foolish. And I have always wished that for myself. And now, as you graduate to begin anew, I wish that for you.

Stay Hungry. Stay Foolish.

Thank you all very much.

Words and Expressions Check-Up

✓ **Reed College** Reed College is a private, independent, liberal arts college located in southeast Portland, Oregon. Founded in 1908, Reed is a four-year residential college with a campus located in Portland's residential Eastmoreland neighborhood, featuring architecture based on the Tudor-Gothic style, and a forested canyon wilderness preserve at its center. Reed is distinctively known for its mandatory freshman humanities program, as the only private undergraduate college with a nuclear reactor supporting its science programs, and for the unusually high percentage of graduates who go on to earn PhDs and other postgraduate degrees. (www.wikipedia.org)

drop-in *noun* a person who or thing that pays an unexpected or uninvited visit: *a feeder for squirrels, raccoons, and other drop-ins.*

drop-out *phrasal verb* to stop attending school or college.

✓ **Hare Krishna Food for Life** The world's largest vegan and vegetarian non-profit food relief organization with projects in over 60 countries. Volunteers serve more than 1,500,000 free meals daily in a variety of ways, including: food vans serving to the homeless within major cities around the world; lunch time meals for poor school children throughout India; and also in response to large natural disasters, such as the 2004 Indian Ocean earthquake. With roots in India, the Food for Life project is a modern day revival of the ancient Vedic culture of hospitality with its belief in the equality of all beings. It was conceived of and began by the International Society for Krishna Consciousness in 1974 and is thus commonly known as *Hare Krishna Food for Life*. It has been lauded by the New York Times and the International Rescue Committee for its relief efforts worldwide. (www.wikipedia.org)

✓ **calligraphy** *noun* (from Greek "beauty" + "writing") is a type of visual art. It is often called the art of writing. A contemporary definition of calligraphic practice is "the art of giving form to signs in an expressive, harmonious and skillful manner". The story of writing is one of aesthetic evolution framed within the technical skills, transmission speed(s) and materials limitations of a person, time and place. A style of writing is described as a script, hand or alphabet.(www.wikipedia.org)

serif *noun* A type of font like AaBbCc.

✓ **Macintosh** Macintosh, or Mac, is a series of several lines of personal computers designed, developed, and marketed by Apple Inc. The Macintosh was introduced on January 24, 1984; it was the first commercially successful personal computer to feature a mouse and a graphical user interface rather than a command-line interface.(www.wikipedia.org)

gut *noun (pl.)* courage and fortitude, nerve, determination, stamina: *Climbing that cliff takes a lot of guts.*

karma *noun* In Hinduism, Buddhism. actions seen as bringing upon oneself inevitable results, good or bad, either in this life or in a reincarnation.

screw up *phrasal verb* to ruin through bungling or stupidity: *Somehow the engineers screwed up the entire construction project.*

start over *phrasal verb* to begin again: *This article is no good. I'll have to start over.*

✓ **Toy Story** Toy Story is a 1995 American computer-animated family/buddy film, directed by John Lasseter and featuring the voices of Tom Hanks and Tim Allen. The film was produced by Pixar Animation Studios and was distributed by Buena Vista Distribution. It was written by Joss Whedon, Andrew Stanton, Joel Cohen, and Alec Sokolow, and featured music by Randy Newman. It was the first feature film released to use only computer-generated imagery. (www.wikipedia.org)

✓ **Pixar** Pixar Animation Studios A CGI animation production company based in Emeryville, California, United States. To date, the studio has earned twenty-two Academy Awards, four Golden Globes, and three Grammys, among many other awards, acknowledgments and achievements. It is one of the most critically acclaimed film studios of all time. It is best known for its CGI-animated feature films which are created with PhotoRealistic RenderMan, its own implementation of the industry-standard Renderman image-rendering API used to generate high-quality images.(www.wikipedia.org)

pancreas *noun* The pancreas is a gland organ in the digestive and endocrine system of vertebrates. It is both an endocrine gland producing several important hormones, including insulin, glucagon, and somatostatin, as well as an exocrine gland, secreting pancreatic juice containing digestive enzymes that pass to the small intestine.

button up *phrasal verb* to complete successfully, finish: *The report is all buttoned up.*

sedation *noun* the calming of mental excitement or abatement of physiological function by the administration of a drug.

biopsy *noun* the removal for diagnostic study of a piece of tissue from a living body.

sign off *phrasal verb* to cease radio or television broadcasting at the end of the day.

Unscramble the words to complete a sentence.

college/ they/ never/ graduated/ have/ from

night/ the parents/ a call/ in the middle of/ got

pretty/ it was/ that time/ scary/ at

came/ to him/ the knowledge/ back

the course/ I/ to take/ decided

what/ you've/ to find/ love/ got/ is

my affairs/ in order / the teacher/ me/ to get/ suggested

Complete the sentence by filling out the blanks.

지난 학기에 골프 과목을 청강했다.

I ______ _____ ____ golf in the last semester.

Edison은 초등학교를 중퇴했다.

Edison _____ ______ ____ elementary school.

노동자 부모가 대학 등록금을 대기는 쉽지 않았다.

The ______-______ parents could not _______ to support the college tuition.

어제 오랜 친구와 우연히 마주쳤다.

I _______ _____ an old friend of mine.

앞을 내다보기는 어려워도 뒤를 돌아보기는 쉽다.

It's hard to _________ _______while it's easy to _______ ________.

나는 시험을 망쳤다.

I ______ _____ the test.

Listen and Fill in the Blanks.

Reed College at that time ________ perhaps the best calligraphy instruction in the country. Throughout the campus every poster, every________ on every drawer, was beautifully hand calligraphed. Because I had dropped out and didn't _____ ___ take the normal classes, I decided to take a calligraphy class to learn how to do this. I learned about serif and san serif typefaces, about varying the ________ of space between different letter combinations, about what makes great typography ______. It was beautiful, historical, artistically ______ __ ___ ______ that science can't capture, and I found it fascinating.

None of this had even a hope of any practical application in my life. But ten years later, when we were designing the first Macintosh computer, it all ______ ______ to me. And we _______it all into the Mac. It was the first computer with beautiful typography. If I had never dropped in on that single course in college, the Mac ______ ____ never had ______multiple typefaces or proportionally spaced fonts. And since Windows just copied the Mac, it's likely that no personal computer would have them. If I ______ ______ _____, I would have never dropped in on this calligraphy class, and personal computers might not have the wonderful typography that they do. Of course it was impossible to _______ the dots looking forward when I was in college. But it was very, very clear ______ _______ ten years later.

To Develop Critical Thinking

Steve Jobs closed his speech by saying "Stay Hungry. Say foolish." Do you agree with his message to the college graduates or to youngsters in general?

An American Joke

A couple from Montana decided to go to Canada for their holidays one summer. They drove north across the border, stopped at a dinosaur park, then continued northeast. After driving for a couple of days, they realized they were lost. They found a small city, and pulled over to ask a pedestrian for directions. "ey buddy, can you tell us where we are?" The pedestrian smiled, said "Saskatoon, Saskatchewan", and went on his way. The driver turned to his wife and said "Well, we still don't know where we are. He doesn't even speak English."

www.geocities.com/seandlh/jokes.htm

3 Epoch-Making Speeches

Farewell to Baseball Address

delivered on April 27, 1947

by **Babe Ruth**

http://www.youtube.com/watch?v=7_cQ3qNUGBM

Thank you very much, ladies and gentlemen. You know how bad my voice sounds — well it feels just as bad.

You know this baseball game of ours comes up from the youth. That means the boys.

And after you're a boy and grow up to know how to play ball, then you come to the boys you see representing themselves today in your national pastime.

The only real game — I think — in the world is baseball.

As a rule, some people think if you give them a football, or a baseball, or something like that— naturally they're athletes right away.

But you can't do that in baseball.

You've gotta start from way down at the bottom, when you're six or seven years of age. You can't wait until you're fifteen or sixteen. You gotta let it grow up with you. And if you're successful, and you try hard enough, you're bound to come out on top — just like these boys have come to the top now.

There's been so many lovely things said about me, and I'm glad that I've had the opportunity to thank everybody.

Thank you.

Babe Ruth in 1921 from www.wikipedia.org

Complete the Sentence by Filling out the Blank.

어제는 몸이 안 좋아 쉬었다.

Yesterday ______ ______, I got a rest.

왕기초부터 시작해야 한다.

Start from ______ ______ at the _______.

An American Joke

A old man was sitting in the front row at a town meeting, heckling the mayor as he delivered a long speech. Finally the mayor could stand it no longer, so he pointed to the heckler and said, "will that gentleman please stand up and tell the audience what he has ever done for the good of the city." "Well Mr. Mayor," the man said in a firm voice. "I voted against you in the last election."

www.jokesaboutamericans.com

Epoch-Making Speeches

4 Epoch-Making Speeches

I Have a Dream

delivered on August 28, 1963

by **Martin Luther King, Jr.**

http://www.youtube.com/watch?v=PbUtL_0vAJk

I am happy to join with you today in what will go down in history as the greatest demonstration for freedom in the history of our nation.

Five score years ago, a great American, in whose symbolic shadow we stand today, signed the Emancipation Proclamation. This momentous decree came as a great beacon light of hope to millions of Negro slaves, who had been seared in the flames of withering injustice. It came as a joyous daybreak to end the long night of their captivity.

But one hundred years later, the Negro still is not free. One hundred years later, the life of the Negro is still sadly crippled by the manacles of segregation and the chains of discrimination. One hundred years later, the Negro lives on a lonely island of poverty in the midst of a vast ocean of material prosperity. One hundred years later, the Negro is still languished in the corners of American society and finds himself an exile in his own land. And so we've come here today to dramatize a shameful condition.

In a sense we have come to our nation's capital to cash a check. When the architects of our republic wrote the magnificent words of the Constitution and the Declaration of Independence, they were signing a promissory note to which every American was to fall heir. This note was a promise that all men, yes, black men as well as white men, would be guaranteed the unalienable rights of life, liberty, and the pursuit of happiness. It is obvious today that America has defaulted on this promissory note, insofar as her citizens of color are concerned. Instead of honoring this sacred obligation, America has given the Negro people a bad check, a check which has come back marked "insufficient funds."

But we refuse to believe that the bank of justice is bankrupt. We refuse to believe that there are insufficient funds in the great vaults of opportunity of this nation. And so we have come to cash this check, a check that will give us upon demand the riches of freedom and the security of justice.

We have also come to this hallowed spot to remind America of the fierce urgency of Now. This is no time to engage in the luxury of cooling off or to take the tranquilizing drug of gradualism. Now is the time to make real the promises of democracy. Now is the time to rise from the dark and desolate valley of segregation to the sunlit path of racial justice. Now is the time to lift our nation from the quicksands of racial injustice to the solid rock of brotherhood. Now is the time to make justice a reality for all of God's children.

It would be fatal for the nation to overlook the urgency of the moment. This sweltering summer of the Negro's legitimate discontent will not pass until there is an invigorating autumn of freedom and equality. Nineteen sixty-three is not an end but a beginning. Those who hope that the Negro needed to blow off steam and will now be content will have a rude awakening if the nation returns to business as usual. There will be neither rest nor tranquility in America until the Negro is granted

March on Washington in 1963
from www.wikipedia.org

his citizenship rights. The whirlwinds of revolt will continue to shake the foundations of our nation until the bright day of justice emerges.

But there is something that I must say to my people who stand on the warm threshold which leads into the palace of justice. In the process of gaining our rightful place we must not be guilty of wrongful deeds. Let us not seek to satisfy our thirst for freedom by drinking from the cup of bitterness and hatred. We must ever conduct our struggle on the high plane of dignity and discipline. We must not allow our creative protest to degenerate into physical violence. Again and again we must rise to the majestic heights of meeting physical force with soul force.

The marvelous new militancy which has engulfed the Negro community must not lead us to a distrust of all white people, for many of our white brothers, as evidenced by their presence here today, have come to realize that their destiny is tied up with our destiny. And they have come to realize that their freedom is inextricably bound to our freedom. We cannot walk alone.

And as we walk, we must make the pledge that we shall always march ahead. We cannot turn back. There are those who are asking the devotees of civil rights, "When will you be satisfied?" We can never be satisfied as long as the Negro is the victim of the unspeakable horrors of police brutality. We can never be satisfied as long as our bodies, heavy with the fatigue of travel, cannot gain lodging in the motels of the highways and the hotels of the cities. We cannot be satisfied as long as a

Negro in Mississippi cannot vote and a Negro in New York believes he has nothing for which to vote. No, no, we are not satisfied and we will not be satisfied until justice rolls down like waters and righteousness like a mighty stream.

I am not unmindful that some of you have come here out of great trials and tribulations. Some of you have come fresh from narrow jail cells. Some of you have come from areas where your quest for freedom left you battered by the storms of persecutions and staggered by the winds of police brutality. You have been the veterans of creative suffering. Continue to work with the faith that unearned suffering is redemptive. Go back to Mississippi, go back to Alabama, go back to South Carolina, go back to Georgia, go back to Louisiana, go back to the slums and ghettos of our northern cities, knowing that somehow this situation can and will be changed. Let us not wallow in the valley of despair, I say to you today, my friends. And so even though we face the difficulties of today and tomorrow, I still have a dream. It is a dream deeply rooted in the American dream.

❧ ❧ ❧ ❧ ❧ ❧

I have a dream that one day this nation will rise up and live out the true meaning of its creed: We hold these truths to be self-evident that all men are created equal.

I have a dream that one day on the red hills of Georgia the sons of former slaves and the sons of former slave owners will be able to sit down together at the table of brotherhood.

I have a dream that one day even the state of Mississippi, a state sweltering with the heat of injustice, sweltering with the heat of oppression, will be transformed into an oasis of freedom and justice.

I have a dream that my four little children will one day live in a nation where they will not be judged by the color of their skin but by the content of their character. I have a *dream* today!

I have a dream that one day, down in Alabama, with its vicious racists, with its governor having his lips dripping with the words of interposition and nullification; one day right down in Alabama little black boys and black girls will be able to join hands with little white boys and white girls as sisters and brothers. I have a dream today!

I have a dream that one day every valley shall be exalted, and every hill and mountain shall be made low, the rough places will be made plain, and the crooked places will be made straight, and the glory of the Lord shall be revealed and all flesh shall see it together.

This is our hope. This is the faith that I will go back to the South with. With this faith we will be able to hew out of the mountain of despair a stone of hope. With this faith we will be able to transform the jangling discords of our nation into a beautiful symphony of brotherhood. With this faith we will be able to work together, to pray together, to struggle together, to go to jail together, to stand up for freedom together, knowing that we will be free one day. And this will be the day, this will be the day when all of God's children will be able to sing with new meaning, "My country 'tis of thee, sweet land of liberty, of thee I sing. Land where my fathers died, land of the Pilgrim's pride, from every mountainside, let freedom ring!" And if America is to be a great nation, this must become true.

And so let freedom ring — from the prodigious hilltops of New Hampshire.

Let freedom ring — from the mighty mountains of New York.

Let freedom ring — from the heightening Alleghenies of Pennsylvania.

Let freedom ring — from the snow-capped Rockies of Colorado.

Let freedom ring — from the curvaceous slopes of California.

But not only that.

Let freedom ring — from Stone Mountain of Georgia.

Let freedom ring — from Lookout Mountain of Tennessee.

Let freedom ring — from every hill and molehill of Mississippi, from every mountainside, let freedom ring!

And when this happens, when we allow freedom to ring, when we let it ring from every village and every hamlet, from every state and every city, we will be able to speed up that day when *all* of God's children, black men and white men, Jews and Gentiles, Protestants and Catholics, will be able to join hands and sing in the words of the old Negro spiritual,

"Free at last, free at last.

Thank *God* Almighty, we are free at last."

Words and Expressions Check-Up

✓ **Emancipation Proclamation** The Emancipation Proclamation consists of two executive orders issued by United States President Abraham Lincoln during the American Civil War. The first one, issued September 22, 1862, declared the freedom of all slaves in any state of the Confederate States of America that did not return to Union control by January 1, 1863. The second order, issued January 1, 1863, named ten specific states where it would apply. Lincoln issued the Executive Order by his authority as "Commander in Chief of the Army and Navy" under Article II, section 2 of the United States Constitution. The Proclamation declared *"that all persons held as slaves are, and henceforward shall be free."* This is saying that there were more limitation than you may think to the Emancipation Proclamation. Some of these limitations were that it only applied to the states that had taken themselves out of the Union. It did not end slavery. But it did cause Americans to feel some sympathy and even empathy. (www.wikipedia.org)

sear *verb* to burn or scorch injuriously or painfully: *He seared his hand on a hot steam pipe.*

manacle *noun* a shackle for the hand, handcuff.

languish *verb* to lose vigor and vitality.

✓ **Declaration of Independence** The United States Declaration of Independence is a statement adopted by the Continental Congress on July 4, 1776, which announced that the thirteen American colonies then at war with Great Britain were now independent states, and thus no longer a part of the British Empire. Written primarily by Thomas Jefferson, the Declaration is a formal explanation of why Congress had voted on July 2 to declare independence from Great Britain, more than a year after the outbreak of the American Revolutionary War. The birthday of the United States of America — Independence Day — is celebrated on July 4, the day the wording of the Declaration was approved by Congress.(www.wikipedia.org)

promissory note *noun* a written promise to pay a specified sum of money to a designated person or to his or her order.

default *verb* to fail to perform or pay: *to default a debt.*

hallowed *adjective* regarded as holy, sacred: *Our father in heaven, Hallowed be thy name.*

blow off steam *idiom* to give vent to one's repressed emotions by talking or behaving in an unrestrained manner: *Don't take her comments too seriously. She was just blowing off steam.*

engulf *verb* to swallow up, submerge: *The flooding water has engulfed many small towns along the river banks.*

redemptive *adjective* of, pertaining to redemption or salvation.

ghetto *noun* a section of a city, densely populated slum area, inhabited predominantly by poor people.

interposition *noun* the doctrine that an individual state of the U.S. may oppose any federal action it believes encroaches on its sovereignty.

nullification *noun* the failure or refusal of a U.S. state to aid in enforcement of federal laws within its limits on Constitutional grounds.

unearned *adjective* not received in exchange for labor or services.

hew *verb* to strike forcibly with an ax, sword, or other cutting instrument.

curvaceous *adjective* having a well-shaped figure with voluptuous curves.

Unscramble the words to complete a sentence.

the horrible living/ it is urgent/ condition/ to dramatize

a reality/ justice/ now/ is the time/ to make.

the urgency/ it would/ to overlook/ be fatal

is/ bound/ their freedom/ to our freedom/ inextricably

should/ be/ of their character/ but/ judged/ not/ by their color/ of their skin/ men/ by the content

can/ freedom/ this faith/ we/ with/ stand up for/ together

Complete the sentence by filling out the blanks.

그들의 삶은 가난 때문에 절름발이가 되었다.

Their lives _____ ______ by the poverty.

상품권을 현금으로 바꿀 수 있다.

It is possible to ______ the vouchers.

지금은 끝이 아니라 시작이다.

Now is not an ______ but a _________.

엄청난 해일이 그 집과 사람들을 삼켜 버렸다.
The enormous tsunami ________ the house and residents.

그들의 미래는 우리의 미래와 뗄 수 없는 관계를 맺고 있다.

Their future is _____ ______ with our future.

부당하게 받은 고통은 보상을 받는다.

_______ suffering is ________.

그의 둘째 아들이 후계자가 될 것이다.

His second son is likely to _____ ______.

Listen and Fill in the Blanks.

Five score years ago, a great American, in _______ symbolic shadow we stand today, signed the Emancipation Proclamation. This momentous decree came as a great _____ _____ of hope to millions of Negro slaves, who had been seared in the flames of withering injustice. It came as a joyous daybreak to _____ the long night of their captivity.

But one hundred years later, the Negro still is not free. One hundred years later, the life of the Negro is still sadly crippled by the manacles of _______ and the chains of discrimination. One hundred years later, the Negro lives on a lonely island of poverty ___ ____ _____ ___ a vast ocean of material prosperity. One hundred years later, the Negro is still languished in the corners of American society and ______ himself an exile in his own land. And so we've come here today to _______ a shameful condition.

In a sense we have come to our nation's capital to _____ a check. When the architects of our republic wrote the magnificent words of the Constitution and the Declaration of Independence, they were _____ a promissory note to which every American was to ____ _____. This note was a promise that all men, yes, black men as well as white men, would be guaranteed the _________ rights of life, liberty, and the pursuit of happiness. It is obvious today that America has ______ on this promissory note, insofar as her citizens of color are concerned. Instead of honoring this sacred obligation, America has given the Negro people a bad check, a check which _____ _____ ______ marked "insufficient funds."

To Develop Critical Thinking

The tone of the speech is radical and seems to instigate the movements of black people. Do you agree with this type of leadership to resolve deep-rooted social or political issues?

An American Joke

A shopkeeper was dismayed when a brand new business much like his own opened up next door and erected a huge sign which read 'BEST DEALS.' He was horrified when another competitor opened up on his right, and announced its arrival with an even larger sign, reading 'LOWEST PRICES.' The shopkeeper panicked, until he got an idea. He put the biggest sign of all over his own shop. It read 'MAIN ENTRANCE'.

www.jokesaboutamericans.com/american_joke_four.html

Gustave Boulanger's painting The Slave Market (www.wikipedia.org)

Epoch-Making Speeches

On Consitution

delivered on September 17, 1787

by **Benjamin Franklin**

http://www.usconstitution.net/franklin.html

Mr. President:

I confess that there are several parts of this constitution which I do not at present approve, but I am not sure I shall never approve them; for having lived long, I have experienced many instances of being obliged by better information, or fuller consideration, to change opinions even on important subjects, which I once thought right, but found to be otherwise. It is therefore that the older I grow, the more apt I am to doubt my own judgment, and to pay more respect to the judgment of others.

Most men indeed as well as most sects in Religion, think themselves in possession of all truth, and that wherever others differ from them it is so far error. Steele a Protestant in a Dedication tells the Pope, that the only difference between our Churches in their opinions of the certainty of their doctrines is, the Church of Rome is infallible and the Church of England is *never* in the wrong. But though many private persons think almost as highly of their own *infallibility* as of that of their sect, few express it so naturally as a certain French lady, who in a dispute with her sister, said "I don't know how it happens, Sister but I meet with no body but myself, that's always in the right. "Je ne trouve que moi qui aie toujours raison."

In these sentiments, Sir, I agree to this Constitution with all its faults, if they are such; because I think a general Government necessary for us, and there is no form of Government but what may be a blessing to the people if well administered, and believe farther that this is likely to be well administered for a course of years, and can only end in Despotism, as other forms have done before it, when the people shall become so corrupted as to need despotic Government, being incapable of any other.

I doubt too whether any other Convention we can obtain, may be able to make a better Constitution. For when you assemble a number of men to have the advantage of their joint wisdom, you inevitably assemble with those men, all their prejudices, their passions, their errors of opinion, their local interests, and their selfish views. From such an assembly can a *perfect* production be expected? It therefore astonishes me, Sir, to find this system approaching so near to perfection as it does; and I think it will astonish our enemies, who are waiting with confidence to hear that our councils are confounded like those of the Builders of Babel; and that our States are on the point of separation, only to meet hereafter for the purpose of cutting one another's throats.

Thus I consent, Sir, to this Constitution because I expect no better, and because I am not sure, that it is not the best. The opinions I have had of its *errors*, I sacrifice to the public good. I have never whispered a syllable of them abroad. Within these walls they were born, and here they shall die. If every one of us in returning to our Constituents were to report the objections he has had to it, and endeavor to gain partisans in support of them, we might prevent its being generally received, and thereby lose all the salutary effects and great advantages resulting naturally in our favor among foreign Nations as well as among ourselves, from our real or apparent unanimity.

Much of the strength and efficiency of any Government in procuring and securing happiness to the people, depends, on *opinion*, on the general opinion of the goodness of the Government, as well as of the wisdom and integrity of its Governors. I hope therefore that for our own sakes as a part of the people, and for the sake of posterity, we shall act heartily and unanimously in recommending this Constitution (if approved by Congress and confirmed by the Conventions) wherever our influence may extend, and turn our future thoughts and endeavors to the means of having it *well* administered.

On the whole, Sir, I can not help expressing a wish that every member of the Convention who may still have objections to it, would with me, on this occasion doubt a little of his own infallibility, and to make manifest our unanimity, put his name to this instrument.

one hundred dollar bill of the US

Words and Expressions Check-Up

despotic *adjective* of, pertaining to, or of the nature of a despot or despotism.

✓ Tower of Babel

The Tower of Babel by Pieter Brueghel the Elder (1563). from www.wikipedia.org

constituent *noun* a person who authorizes another to act in his/ her behalf.
procure *verb* to obtain or get by care, effort, or the use of special means.
instrument *noun* a formal legal document.
partisan *noun* an adherent or supporter of a person, group, party, or cause.

Unscramble the words to complete a sentence.

from/ can/ perfect production/ be expected/ such an assembly?

seeks/ constantly/ the congressman/ partisans/ to gain

Complete the sentence by filling out the blanks.

나이를 먹을수록 내 판단력을 의심하게 되었다.

_____ ______ I grow, _____ _____ apt I am to doubt my judgement.

잘 알고 보니 내 생각이 잘못되었더라.

By _______ _______, my opinions _______ to be incorrect.

Listen and Fill in the Blanks.

I confess that there are several _______ of this constitution which I do not ___ _______ ______, but I am not sure I shall never ______ them; for having lived long, I have experienced many instances of being ______ by ______ _________, or ______ _________, to change opinions even on important subjects, which I once thought _______, but found to be _______. It is therefore that the older I grow, the more apt I am to _______ my own judgment, and to _____ more ______ to the judgment of others.

To Develop Critical Thinking

Benjamin Franklin confessed that he did not like to listen to others when he was young, and only in his elderly years did he start to listen to others. Are you personally a good listener, and how do you think about listening in communication?

Legacy by Ben Franklin

- Speak not but what may benefit others or yourself, avoid trifling conversation.
- Make no expense but to be good to yourself, i.e., waste nothing.
- Avoid extremes; forebear resenting injuries so much you think they deserve.
- Lose no time; be always employ'd in something useful; cut off all unnecessary actions.
- We must all hang together or assuredly well all hang separately.
- A learned blockhead is a greater blockhead than an ignorant one.
- Either write things worthy of reading, or do things worth the writing.
- A penny saved is twopence dear.
- Fish and visitors smell after three days.
- Beware of the young doctor and the old barber.

(www.wikipedia.org)

Checks and Balances

The separation of powers, also known as trias politica, is a model for the governance of democratic states. The model was first developed in ancient Greece and came into widespread use by the Roman Republic as part of the uncodified Constitution of the Roman Republic. Under this model, the state is divided into branches or estates, each with separate and independent powers and areas of responsibility. The normal division of estates is into an executive, a legislature, and a judiciary. The opposite of separation of powers is the fusion of powers, often a feature of parliamentary democracies. In this form, the executive, which often consists of a prime minister and cabinet ("government"), is drawn from the legislature (parliament). This is the principle of responsible government. However, although the legislative and executive branches are connected, in parliamentary systems there is usually an independent judiciary and the government's role in the parliament does not give them unlimited legislative influence.

(www.wikipedia.org)

An American Joke

Q: Why does it take 3 Americans to change a lightbulb?
A: One to stand on the ladder, and two to carry enough lightbulbs until one is found that isn't defective.

Q: How can you tell it's midnight at an American airport?
A: When you see the 8:00 PM flights taking off.

Q: What do Americans call a TV set that goes five years without need of repair?
A: An import.

Q: How can an American be certain that the car he's just bought is actually new?
A: When it's recalled by the factory.

www.jokesaboutamericans.com/american_joke_four.html

Epoch-Making Speeches

Harvard University Commencement Speech

delivered on June 7, 2007.

by **Bill Gates**

http://www.youtube.com/watch?v=-Uz92tcEXtY

Moderator: After a thirty-three-year-leave of absence from his alma mater, I am pleased to present you Doctor William Gates.

President Bok, former President Rudenstine, incoming President Faust, members of the Harvard Corporation and the Board of Overseers, members of the faculty, parents, and especially, the graduates:

I've been waiting more than 30 years to say this: "Dad, I always told you I'd come back and get my degree."

I want to thank Harvard for this honor. I'll be changing my job next year … and it will be nice to finally have a college degree on my resume.

I applaud the graduates today for taking a much more direct route to your degrees. For my part, I'm just happy that the Crimson has called me "Harvard's most successful dropout." I guess that makes me valedictorian of my own special class ... I did the best of everyone who failed.

But I also want to be recognized as the guy who got Steve Ballmer to drop out of business school. I'm a bad influence. That's why I was invited to speak at your graduation. If I had spoken at your orientation, fewer of you might be here today.

Harvard was just a phenomenal experience for me. Academic life was fascinating. I used to sit in on lots of classes I hadn't even signed up for. And dorm life was terrific. I lived up at Radcliffe, in Currier House. There were always lots of people in my dorm room late at night discussing things, because everyone knew I didn't worry about getting up in the morning. That's how I came to be the leader of the anti-social group. We clung to each other as a way of validating our rejection of all those social people.

Radcliffe was a great place to live. There were more women up there, and most of the guys were science-math types. That combination offered me the best odds, if you know what I mean. This is where I learned the sad lesson that improving your odds doesn't guarantee success.

One of my biggest memories of Harvard came in January 1975, when I made a call from Currier House to a company in Albuquerque, New Mexico that had begun making the world's first personal computers. I offered to sell them software.

I worried that they would realize I was just a student in a dorm and hang up on me. Instead they said: "We're not quite ready, come see us in a month," which was a good thing, because we hadn't written the software yet. From that moment, I worked day and night on this little extra credit project that marked the end of my college education and the beginning of a remarkable journey with Microsoft.

What I remember above all about Harvard was being in the midst of so much energy and intelligence. It could be exhilarating, intimidating, sometimes even discouraging, but always challenging. It was an amazing privilege – and though I left early, I was transformed by my years at Harvard, the friendships I made, and the ideas I worked on.

But taking a serious look back … I do have one big regret.

I left Harvard with no real awareness of the awful inequities in the world – the appalling disparities of health, and wealth, and opportunity that condemn millions of people to lives of despair.

I learned a lot here at Harvard about new ideas in economics and politics. I got great exposure to the advances being made in the sciences.

But humanity's greatest advances are not in its discoveries — but in how those discoveries are applied to reduce inequity. Whether through democracy, strong public education, quality health care, or broad economic opportunity — reducing inequity is the highest human achievement.

I left campus knowing little about the millions of young people cheated out of educational opportunities here in this country. And I knew nothing about the millions of people living in unspeakable poverty and disease in developing countries.

It took me decades to find out.

You graduates came to Harvard at a different time. You know more about the world's inequities than the classes that came before. In your years here, I hope you've had a chance to think about how — in this age of accelerating technology we can finally take on these inequities, and we can solve them.

Imagine, just for the sake of discussion, that you had a few hours a week and a few dollars a month to donate to a cause — and you wanted to spend that time and money where it would have the greatest impact in saving and improving lives. Where would you spend it?

For Melinda and for me, the challenge is the same: how can we do the most good for the greatest number with the resources we have.

During our discussions on this question, Melinda and I read an article about the millions of children who were dying every year in poor countries from diseases that we had long ago made harmless in this country. Measles, malaria, pneumonia, hepatitis B, yellow fever. One disease I had never even heard of, rotavirus, was killing half a million children each year — none of them in the United States.

We were shocked. We had just assumed that if millions of children were dying and they could be saved, the world would make it a priority to discover and deliver the medicines to save them. But it did not. For under a dollar, there were interventions that could save lives that just weren't being delivered.

If you believe that every life has equal value, it's revolting to learn that some lives are seen as worth saving and others are not. We said to ourselves: "This can't be true. But if it is true, it deserves to be the priority of our giving."

So we began our work in the same way anyone here would begin it. We asked: "How could the world let these children die?"

Harvard Yard with freshman dorms in the background (www.wikipedia.org)

The answer is simple, and harsh. The market did not reward saving the lives of these children, and governments did not subsidize it. So the children died because their mothers and their fathers had no power in the market and no voice in the system.

But you and I have both.

We can make market forces work better for the poor if we can develop a more creative capitalism — if we can stretch the reach of market forces so that more people can make a profit, or at least make a living, serving people who are suffering from the great inequities. We also can press governments around the world to spend taxpayer money in ways that better reflect the values of the people who pay the taxes.

If we can find approaches that meet the needs of the poor in ways that generate profits for business and votes for politicians, we will have found a sustainable way to reduce inequity in the world. This task is open-ended. It can never be finished. But a conscious effort to answer this challenge will change the world.

I am optimistic that we can do this, but I talk to skeptics who claim there is no hope. They say: "Inequity has been with us since the beginning, and will be with us till the end — because people just … don't … care." I completely disagree.

Widener Library (from www.wikipedia.org)

I believe we have more caring than we know what to do with.

All of us here in this Yard, at one time or another, have seen human tragedies that broke our hearts, and yet we did nothing — not because we didn't care, but because we didn't know what to do. If we had known how to help, we would have acted.

The barrier to change is not too little caring; it is too much complexity.

To turn caring into action, we need to see a problem, see a solution, and see the impact. But complexity blocks all three steps.

Even with the advent of the Internet and 24-hour news, it is still a complex enterprise to get people to truly see the problems. When an airplane crashes, officials immediately call a press conference. They promise to investigate, determine the cause, and prevent similar crashes in the future.

But if the officials were brutally honest, they would say: "Of all the people in the world who died today from preventable causes, one half of one percent of them were on this plane. We're determined to do everything possible to solve the problem that took the lives of the one half of one percent."

The bigger problem is not the plane crash, but the millions of preventable deaths.

We don't read much about these deaths. The media covers what's new — and millions of people dying is nothing new. So it stays in the background, where it's easier to ignore. But even when we do see it or read about it, it's difficult to keep our eyes on the problem. It's hard to look at suffering if the situation is so complex that we don't know how to help. And so we look away.

If we can really see a problem, which is the first step, we come to the second step: cutting through the complexity to find a solution.

Finding solutions is essential if we want to make the most of our caring.

If we have clear and proven answers anytime an organization or individual asks "How can I help?," then we can get action — and we can make sure that none of the caring in the world is wasted. But complexity makes it hard to mark a path of action for everyone who cares — and that makes it hard for their caring to matter.

Cutting through complexity to find a solution runs through four predictable stages: determine a goal, find the highest-leverage approach, discover the ideal technology for that approach, and in the meantime, make the smartest application of the technology that you already have — whether it's something sophisticated, like a new drug, or something simpler, like a bednet.

The AIDS epidemic offers an example. The broad goal, of course, is to end the disease. The highest-impact approach is prevention. The ideal technology would be a vaccine that gives lifetime immunity with a single dose. So governments, drug companies, and foundations are funding vaccine research. But their work is likely to take more than a decade, so in the meantime, we have to work with what we have in hand — and the best prevention approach we have now is getting people to avoid risky behavior.

Pursuing that goal starts the four-step cycle again. This is the pattern. The crucial thing is to never stop thinking and working — and never do what we did with malaria and tuberculosis in the 20th century — which is to surrender to complexity and quit.

The final step — after seeing the problem and finding an approach — is to measure the impact of your work and share your successes and failures so that others learn from your efforts.

You have to have the statistics, of course. You have to be able to show that a program is vaccinating millions more children. You have to be able to show an example of decline in the number of children dying from these diseases. This is essential not just to improve the program, but also to help draw more investment from business and government.

But if you want to inspire people to participate, you have to show more than numbers; you have to convey the human impact of the work — so people can feel what saving a life means to the families affected.

I remember going to the World Economic Forum some years back and sitting on a global health panel that was discussing ways to save millions of lives. Millions! Think of the thrill that you can save just one person's life — then multiply that by millions. ... Yet this was the most boring panel I've ever been on — ever. So boring even I couldn't stand it.

What made that experience especially striking was that I had just come from an event where we were introducing version 13 of some piece of software, and we had people jumping and shouting with excitement. I love getting people excited about software — but why can't we generate even more excitement for saving lives?

You can't get people excited unless you can help them see and feel the impact. And the way you do that — is a complex question.

Still, I'm optimistic. Yes, inequity has been with us forever, but the new tools we have to cut through complexity have not been with us forever. They are new — they can help us make the most of our caring — and that's why the future can be different from the past.

The defining and ongoing innovations of this age — biotechnology, the personal computer, the Internet — give us a chance we've never had before to end extreme poverty and end death from preventable disease.

Sixty years ago, George Marshall came to this commencement and announced a plan to assist the nations of post-war Europe. He said: "I think one difficulty is that the problem is one of such enormous complexity that the very mass of facts presented to the public by press and radio make it exceedingly difficult for the man in the street to reach a clear appraisement of the situation. It is virtually impossible at this distance to grasp at all the real significance of the situation."

Thirty years after Marshall made his address, as my class graduated without me, technology was emerging that would make the world smaller, more open, more visible, less distant.

The emergence of low-cost personal computers gave rise to a powerful network that has transformed opportunities for learning and communicating.

The magical thing about this network is not just that it collapses distance and makes everyone your neighbor. It also dramatically increases the number of brilliant minds we can have working together on the same problem — and that scales up the rate of innovation to a staggering degree.

At the same time, for every person in the world who has access to this technology, five people don't. That means many creative minds are left out of this discussion — smart people with practical intelligence and relevant experience who don't have the technology to hone their talents or contribute their ideas to the world.

We need as many people as possible to gain access to this technology, because these advances are triggering a revolution in what human beings can do for one another. They are making it possible not just for national governments, but for universities, corporations, smaller organizations, and even individuals to see problems, see approaches, and measure the impact of their efforts to address the hunger, poverty, and desperation George Marshall spoke of 60 years ago.

Members of the Harvard Family: Here in the Yard is one of the great collections of intellectual talent in the world.

For what purpose?

There is no question that the faculty, the alumni, the students, and the benefactors of Harvard have used their power to improve the lives of people here and around the world. But can we do more? Can Harvard dedicate its intellect to improving the lives of people who will never even hear its name?

Let me make a request of the deans and the professors — the intellectual leaders here at Harvard: As you hire new faculty, award tenure, review curriculum, and determine degree requirements, please ask yourselves:

Should our best minds be dedicated to solving our biggest problems?

Should Harvard encourage its faculty to take on the world's worst inequities? Should Harvard students learn about the depth of global poverty ... the prevalence of world hunger ... the scarcity of clean water ...the girls kept out of school ... the children who die from diseases we can cure?

Should the world's most privileged people learn about the lives of the world's least privileged?

These are not rhetorical questions — you will answer with your policies.

My mother, who was filled with pride the day I was admitted here — never stopped pressing me to do more for others. A few days before I was married, she hosted a bridal event, at which she read aloud a letter about marriage that she had written to Melinda. My mother was very ill with cancer at the time, but she saw one more opportunity to deliver her message, and at the close of the letter she said: "From those to whom much is given, much is expected."

When you consider what those of us here in this Yard have been given — in talent, privilege, and opportunity — there is almost no limit to what the world has a right to expect from us.

In line with the promise of this age, I want to exhort each of the graduates here to take on an issue — a complex problem, a deep inequity, and become a specialist on it. If you make it the focus of your career, that would be phenomenal. But you don't have to do that to make an impact. For a few hours every week, you can use the growing power of the Internet to get informed, find others with the same interests, see the barriers, and find ways to cut through them.

Don't let complexity stop you. Be activists. Take on the big inequities. I feel sure it will be one of the great experiences of your lives.

You graduates are coming of age in an amazing time. As you leave Harvard, you have technology that members of my class never had. You have awareness of global inequity, which we did not have. And with that awareness, you likely also have an informed conscience that will torment you if you abandon these people whose lives you could change with very modest effort. You have more than we had; you must start sooner, and carry on longer.

And I hope you will come back here to Harvard 30 years from now and reflect on what you have done with your talent and your energy. I hope you will judge yourselves not on your professional accomplishments alone, but also on how well you have addressed the world's deepest inequities ... on how well you treated people a world away who have nothing in common with you but their humanity.

Good luck.

Words and Expressions Check-Up

applaud *verb* to clap the hands as an expression of approval, appreciation, acclamation.

✓ **Harvard Crimson** Crimson is a strong, bright, deep red color combined with some blue, resulting in a tiny degree of purple. It is originally the color of the dye produced from a scale insect, *Kermes vermilio*, but the name is now also used for slightly bluish-red colors in general that are between red and rose. (www.wikipedia.org)

valedictorian *noun* a student, usually the one ranking highest academically in a school graduating class, who delivers the valedictory at the commencement.

✓ **Steve Ballmer** Steven Anthony Ballmer is an American businessman who has been the chief executive officer of Microsoft Corporation since January 2000. Ballmer is the second person after Roberto Goizueta to become a billionaire in U.S. dollars based on stock options received as an employee of a corporation in which he was neither a founder nor a relative of a founder. In Forbes 2008 World' s Richest People ranking, Ballmer was ranked the 43rd richest person in the world, with an estimated wealth of $11 billion.(www.wikipedia.org)

phenomenal *adjective* uncommon, outstanding, surpassing, unprecedented.

sit in on *idiom* to be a spectator, observer, or visitor at: *to sit in on classes.*

✓ **Radcliffe** Radcliffe College was a women's liberal arts college in Cambridge, Massachusetts, and was the coordinate college for Harvard University. It was also one of the Seven Sisters colleges. Radcliffe College conferred joint Harvard-Radcliffe diplomas beginning in 1963 and a formal merger agreement with Harvard was signed in 1977, with full integration with Harvard completed in 1999. Today, Radcliffe's campus functions as a research institute within Harvard, the Radcliffe Institute for Advanced Study, and former Radcliffe student housing has been incorporated as residential houses of Harvard College.(www.wikipedia.org)

measles *noun* an acute infectious disease occurring mostly in children.

hepatitis B *noun* The hepatitis B virus causes hepatitis B. Viruses are germs that can cause sickness

yellow fever *noun* an acute, often fatal, infectious febrile disease of warm climates, caused by an RNA virus transmitted by a mosquito.

rotavirus *noun* a double-stranded RNA virus of the genus *Rotavirus*, family Reoviridae, that is a major cause of infant diarrhea.

subsidize *verb* to furnish or aid with a subsidy.

inequity *noun* lack of equity, unfairness, favoritism or bias.

exhort *verb* to urge, advise, or caution earnestly admonish urgently.

Unscramble the words to complete a sentence.

we/ night/ the project/ day and/ on/ worked

by/ I/ was/ the school days/ transformed/ the friendships/ and

decades/ me/ to/ it/ find/ took/ out

reach/ we/ the/ of our force/ stretch/ must

background/ the article/ in the/ stayed

efficient/ the highest/ is/ prevention/ approach

the world/ from/ us/ there is/ expect/ no limit/ to what

Complete the sentence by filling out the blanks.

그 아이는 이공계 타입니다.

The guy is an engineering and science ______.

전화 끊지 말고 기다려!

Don't _____ ______, and _______ on the line.

나는 그 대학에서 새로운 학문에 접할 수 있었다.

I was able to get ________ to the new scholarship.

이 질문에 대한 답은 정해져 있지 않다.

The answer to this question is _____-______.

즉시 회의를 소집하자.

Let's ____ a _____ immediately.

우리는 당장 가지고 있는 것으로 작업을 해야 한다.

We have to work with _____ we have ___ ____.

많이 받아본 사람에게 많은 것을 기대할 수 있다.

From those to whom much _____ _____, much _____ _____.

Listen and Fill in the Blanks.

One of my biggest memories of Harvard came in January 1975, when I made a call from Currier House to a company in Albuquerque that had begun making the world's ____ _____ computers. I offered to ____ ___ software. I worried that they would realize I was just a student ___ __ ___ and ___ ___ ___ me. Instead they said: "We're not quite ready, come see us in a month," which was a good thing, because we hadn't written the software yet. From that moment, I worked day and night on this little ____ ___ project that ______ the end of my college education and the beginning of a remarkable ______ with Microsoft.

What I remember above all about Harvard was being ___ ___ ___ ___ so much energy and intelligence. It could be exhilarating, intimidating, sometimes even discouraging, but always ________. It was an amazing _______ —and though I left early, I was transformed by my years at Harvard, the friendships I ______, and the ideas I worked on.

But taking a serious look back … I do have one big regret.

I left Harvard with no real awareness of the awful inequities in the world —the _______ ______ of health, and wealth, and opportunity that ______ millions of people to lives of despair.

I learned a lot here at Harvard about new ideas in economics and politics. I got great exposure to the advances being made in the sciences.

But humanity's greatest ______ are not in its discoveries—but in how those discoveries are applied to reduce ______. Whether through democracy, strong public education, quality health care, or broad economic opportunity—reducing inequity is the highest human achievement.

I left campus knowing little about the millions of young people ______ ____ _____ educational opportunities here in this country. And I knew nothing about the millions of people living in ______ poverty and disease in developing countries.

To Develop Critical Thinking

Bill Gates gave us a clear message: We should strive to get rid of inequity on this planet. In addition, he stressed that a world without inequity should be then ultimate goal for us. Are you sure of the success of this line of efforts?

In personal computers, Ultra-Mobile PC (often abbreviated UMPC) is a term for small form factor (a standard size and shape) for tablet PCs, originally codenamed Project Origami. (www.wikipedia.org)

Lesser Known Facts about Bill Gates

1. Bill Gates earns US$250 every SECOND, that's about US$20 Million a DAY and US$7.8 Billion a YEAR!
2. If he drops a thousand dollars, he won't even bother to pick it up because during the 4 seconds he picks it, he would've already earned it back.
3. The US national debt is about 5.62 trillion dollars, if Bill Gates were to pay the debt by himself; he will finish it in less then 10 years.
4. He can donate US$15 to everyone on earth but still be left with US$5 Million for his pocket money.
5. Michael Jordan is the highest paid athlete in US. If he doesn't drink and eat, and keeps up his annual income i.e. US$30 Million, he'll have to wait for 277 years to become as rich as Bill Gates is now.
6. If Bill Gates was a country, he would be the 37th richest country on earth.
7. If you change all of Bill Gate's money to US$1 notes , you can make a road from the earth to moon, 14 times back and forth. But you have to make that road non-stop for 1,400 years, and use a total of 713 BOEING 747 planes to transport all the money.
8. Bill Gates is 40 this year. If we assume that he will live for another 35 years, he has to spend US$6.78 Million per day to finish all his money before he goes to heaven.

Last but not the least:

The Best One!!

If Microsoft Windows' users can claim US$1 for every time their computers hang because of Microsoft Windows, Bill Gates will be bankrupt in 3 years.

www.jokesaboutamericans.com/american_joke_four.html

7 Epoch-Making Speeches

Inauguration Address

delivered on January 20, 1961

by **John F. Kennedy**

http://www.youtube.com/watch?v=xE0iPY7XGBo&feature=fvst

Vice President Johnson, Mr. Speaker, Mr. Chief Justice, President Eisenhower, Vice President Nixon, President Truman, reverend clergy, fellow citizens:

We observe today not a victory of party, but a celebration of freedom — symbolizing an end, as well as a beginning — signifying renewal, as well as change. For I have sworn before you and Almighty God the same solemn oath our forebears prescribed nearly a century and three-quarters ago.

The world is very different now. For man holds in his mortal hands the power to abolish all forms of human poverty and all forms of human life. And yet the same revolutionary beliefs for which our forebears fought are still at issue around the globe — the belief that the rights of man come not from the generosity of the state, but from the hand of God.

We dare not forget today that we are the heirs of that first revolution. Let the word go forth from this time and place, to friend and foe alike, that the torch has been passed to a new generation of Americans — born in this century, tempered by war, disciplined by a hard and bitter peace, proud of our ancient heritage, and unwilling to witness or permit the slow undoing of those human rights to which this nation has always been committed, and to which we are committed today at home and around the world. Let every nation know, whether it wishes us well or ill, that we shall pay any price, bear any burden, meet any hardship, support any friend, oppose any foe, to assure the survival and the success of liberty.

This much we pledge — and more. To those old allies whose cultural and spiritual origins we share, we pledge the loyalty of faithful friends. United there is little we cannot do in a host of cooperative ventures. Divided there is little we can do — for we dare not meet a powerful challenge at odds and split asunder.

To those new states whom we welcome to the ranks of the free, we pledge our word that one form of colonial control shall not have passed away merely to be replaced by a far more iron tyranny. We shall not always expect to find them supporting our view. But we shall always hope to find them strongly supporting their own freedom — and to remember that, in the past, those who foolishly sought power by riding the back of the tiger ended up inside.

To those people in the huts and villages of half the globe struggling to break the bonds of mass misery, we pledge our best efforts to help them help themselves, for whatever period is required — not because the Communists may be doing it, not because we seek their votes, but because it is right. If a free society cannot help the many who are poor, it cannot save the few who are rich.

John F. Kennedy greets volunteers on August 28, 1961 (from www.wikipedia.org)

To our sister republics south of our border, we offer a special pledge: to convert our good words into good deeds, in a new alliance for progress, to assist free men and free governments in casting off the chains of poverty. But this peaceful revolution of hope cannot become the prey of hostile powers. Let all our neighbors know that we shall join with them to oppose aggression or subversion anywhere in the Americas. And let every other power know that this hemisphere intends to remain the master of its own house.

To that world assembly of sovereign states, the United Nations, our last best hope in an age where the instruments of war have far outpaced the instruments of peace, we renew our pledge of support — to prevent it from becoming merely a forum for invective, to strengthen its shield of the new and the weak, and to enlarge the area in which its writ may run. Finally, to those nations who would make themselves our adversary, we offer not a pledge but a request: that both sides begin anew the quest for peace, before the dark powers of destruction unleashed by science engulf all humanity in planned or accidental self-destruction.

We dare not tempt them with weakness. For only when our arms are sufficient beyond doubt can we be certain beyond doubt that they will never be employed.

But neither can two great and powerful groups of nations take comfort from our present course — both sides overburdened by the cost of modern weapons, both rightly alarmed by the steady spread of the deadly atom, yet both racing to alter that uncertain balance of terror that stays the hand of mankind's final war.

So let us begin anew — remembering on both sides that civility is not a sign of weakness, and sincerity is always subject to proof. Let us never negotiate out of fear, but let us never fear to negotiate.

Let both sides explore what problems unite us instead of belaboring those problems which divide us. Let both sides, for the first time, formulate serious and precise proposals for the inspection and control of arms, and bring the absolute power to destroy other nations under the absolute control of all nations. Let both sides seek to invoke the wonders of science instead of its terrors. Together let us explore the stars, conquer the deserts, eradicate disease, tap the ocean depths, and encourage the arts and commerce. Let both sides unite to heed, in all corners of the earth, the command of Isaiah — to "undo the heavy burdens, and [to] let the oppressed go free." And, if a beachhead of cooperation may push back the jungle of suspicion, let both sides join in creating a new

John F. Kennedy's Presidential Inauguration Ceremony
(from www.wikipedia.org)

endeavor — not a new balance of power, but a new world of law — where the strong are just, and the weak secure, and the peace preserved. All this will not be finished in the first one hundred days. Nor will it be finished in the first one thousand days; nor in the life of this Administration; nor even perhaps in our lifetime on this planet. But let us begin. In your hands, my fellow citizens, more than mine, will rest the final success or failure of our course. Since this country was founded, each generation of Americans has been summoned to give testimony to its national loyalty. The graves of young Americans who answered the call to service surround the globe. Now the trumpet summons us again — not as a call to bear arms, though arms we need — not as a call to battle, though embattled we are — but a call to bear the burden of a long twilight struggle, year in and year out, "rejoicing in hope; patient in tribulation," a struggle against the common enemies of man: tyranny, poverty, disease, and war itself.

1959 in Senate Office (from www.wikipedia.org)

Can we forge against these enemies a grand and global alliance, North and South, East and West, that can assure a more fruitful life for all mankind? Will you join in that historic effort? In the long history of the world, only a few generations have been granted the role of defending freedom in its hour of maximum danger. I do not shrink from this responsibility — I welcome it. I do not believe that any of us would exchange places with any other people or any other generation. The energy, the faith, the devotion which we bring to this endeavor will light our country and all who serve it. And the glow from that fire can truly light the world. And so, my fellow Americans, ask not what your country can do for you; ask what you can do for your country. My fellow citizens of the world, ask not what America will do for you, but what together we can do for the freedom of man.

Finally, whether you are citizens of America or citizens of the world, ask of us here the same high standards of strength and sacrifice which we ask of you. With a good conscience our only sure reward, with history the final judge of our deeds, let us go forth to lead the land we love, asking His blessing and His help, but knowing that here on earth God's work must truly be our own.

Lincoln Bible

The Lincoln Bible was the Bible used by president Abraham Lincoln at his presidential inauguration. The Bible, part of the collection of the Library of Congress was also used by Barack Obama at his inauguration in 2009. The Bible itself is an Oxford University Press edition published in 1853, has 1,280 pages, and measures approximately 15 cm (6 in) in length and 10 cm (4 in) in width, and 4.5 cm in thickness, and is bound in burgundy red velvet with gilt edges. The Bible is due to go on display at the Library of Congress until May 2009 in a celebration of Abraham Lincoln's Bicentennial.

The text and image are adopted from www.wikipeida.org

Words and Expressions Check-Up

at odds *idiom* at variance, in disagreement: *They were usually at odds over political issues.*

asunder *adverb* into separate parts into pieces: *Lightning split the old oak tree asunder.*

invective *noun* vehement or violent denunciation, censure, or reproach.

unleash *verb* to release from or as if from a leash.

belabor *verb* to assail persistently, as with scorn or ridicule: *a book that belabors narrow-mindedness of his contemporaries.*

tap *verb* to draw liquid from a vessel or container.

embattle *verb* to arrange in order of battle, prepare for battle.

Unscramble the words to complete a sentence.

oath/ solemn/ I have/ the same/ before you/ sworn

tempered/ our/ was/ by war/ generation

share/ with/ we /cultural/ those countries/ origins

of poverty/ struggled/ they/ to/ the chains/ cast off

our arms/ the future/ only when/ are sufficient/ can/ we/ be certain about

the success/ will/ in our hands/ rest

you/ not what/ do for/ government/ ask

Complete the sentence by filling out the blanks.

인권은 하나님의 손에서 나온다.

The rights of man _____ _____ the hand of God.

테레사 수녀는 적과 동지를 똑같이 도왔다.

Mother Teresa helped ______ and _______ alike.

우리는 어떠한 대가도 치를 것이다.

We are willing to _____ _____ _____.

사분오열이 되어 적과 맞설 수 없다.

______ ______ we could not appose any foe.

그 사람은 호가호위하면서 권력을 추구한다.

He seeks power by ______ _____ ______ of the tiger.

나는 문제를 너무 오래 물고 늘어지는 경향이 있다.

I tend to________ a problem too long.

날이면 날마다 연습한다.

I practice _____ ___ _____ _____.

Listen and Fill in the Blanks.

To those people in the huts and villages of half the globe ______ to break the bonds of ______ ______, we pledge our best efforts to help them help themselves, for whatever period is required — not because the Communists may be doing it, not because we ______their ______, but because it is right. If a free society cannot help the _____ who are poor, it cannot save the ______ who are rich.

To our _____ republics south of our border, we offer a special pledge: to convert our good _____ into good ______, in a new alliance for progress, to assist free men and free governments in _____ _____ the chains of poverty. But this peaceful revolution of hope cannot become the prey of hostile powers. Let all our neighbors know that we shall join with them to _______ aggression or ______ anywhere in the Americas. And let every other power know that this hemisphere intends to remain the ______ of its own house.

To that world assembly of ______ states, the United Nations, our last best hope in an age where the instruments of war have far _______ the instruments of peace, we renew our pledge of support — to prevent it from becoming merely a forum for invective, to strengthen its shield of the new and the weak, and to enlarge the area in which its ______ may _____.

To Develop Critical Thinking

The time-honored line from President John F. Kennedy's inaugural address is: Ask no what your country can do for you; ask what you can do for your country. However, we have traditionally believed that government exists for the people. Do you agree with the message given in that sentence?

Kennedy and Cuban Missile Crisis

The Cuban Missile Crisis was a confrontation between the United States, the Soviet Union, and Cuba in October 1962, during the Cold War. In Russia, it is termed the "Caribbean Crisis," while in Cuba it is called the "October Crisis." The Cuban and Soviet governments in September 1962 placed nuclear missiles on Cuba. When United States intelligence discovered the weapons its government decided to do all they could to ensure the removal of them. The crisis ranks with the Berlin Blockade as one of the major confrontations of the Cold War, and is generally regarded as the moment in which the Cold War came closest to a nuclear war. (www.wikipedia.org)

Kennedy signs the Proclamation for Interdiction of the Delivery of Offensive Weapons to Cuba at the Oval Office on October 23, 1962.
(from www.wikipedia.org)

An American Joke

The fishing season hasn't opened and a fisherman who doesn't have a license, is casting for trout as a stranger approaches and asks, "Any luck?"

"Any luck? This is a wonderful spot. I took 10 out of this stream yesterday," he boasts.

"Is that so? By the way, do you know who I am?" asks the stranger.

"Nope."

"Well, meet the new game warden."

"Oh," gulped the fisherman. "Well, do you know who I am?"

"Nope."

"Meet the biggest liar in the state."

www.jokesaboutamericans.com/american_joke_four.html

The Sinews of Peace

delivered on March 5, 1946

by **Winston Churchill**

http://www.youtube.com/watch?v=jvax5VUvjWQ

President McCluer, ladies and gentlemen, and last but certainly not least, President of the United States of America:

I am very glad indeed to come to Westminster College this afternoon, and I am complimented that you should give me a degree from an institution whose reputation has been so solidly established. The name "Westminster" somehow or other seems familiar to me. I — I feel as if I've heard of it before. Indeed now that I come to think of it, it was at Westminster that I received a very large part of my education in politics, dialectic, rhetoric — and one or two other things. So, in fact we have both been educated at the same, or similar, or, at any rate, kindred establishments.

It is also an honor, ladies and gentlemen, perhaps almost unique, for a private visitor to be introduced to an academic audience by the President of the United States. Amid his heavy burdens, duties, and responsibilities — unsought but not recoiled from — the President has traveled a thousand miles to dignify and magnify our meeting here today and to give me an opportunity of addressing this kindred nation, as well as my own countrymen across the ocean, and — and perhaps some other countries too. The — The President has told you that it is his wish, as I am sure it is yours, that I should have full liberty to give my true and faithful counsel in these anxious and baffling times. Now, I shall certainly avail myself of this freedom, and feel the more right to do so because any private ambitions I may have cherished in my younger days have been satisfied beyond my wildest dreams. Let me, however, make it clear that I have no official mission or status of any kind, and that I speak only for myself. There is nothing here but what you see.

I can therefore allow my mind, with the experience of a lifetime, to play over the problems which beset us on the morrow of our absolute victory in arms, and to try to make sure with what strength I have that what has been gained with so much sacrifice and suffering shall be preserved for the future glory and safety of mankind.

Ladies and gentlemen, the United States stands at this time at the pinnacle of world power. It is a solemn moment for the American democracy. For with primacy in power is also joined an awe-inspiring accountability to the future. If, as you look around you — If you look around you, you must feel not only the sense of duty done but also you must feel anxiety lest you fall below the level of achievement. Opportunity is here now, clear and shining for both our countries. To reject it or ignore it or fritter it away will bring upon us all the long reproaches of the after-time. It is necessary that constancy of mind, persistency of purpose, and the grand simplicity of decision shall rule and guide the conduct of the English-speaking peoples in peace as they did in war. And we must, and I believe we shall, prove ourselves equal to this severe requirement.

President McCluer, when American military men approach some serious situation they are wont to write at the head of their directive the words "over-all strategic concept." There is wisdom in this, as it leads to clarity of thought. What then is the overall strategic concept which we should inscribe today? It is nothing less than the safety and welfare, the freedom and progress, of all the homes and families of all the men and women in all the lands. And here I speak particularly of the myriad cottage or apartment homes where the wage-earner strives amid the accidents and difficulties of life to guard his wife and children from privation and bring the family up in the fear of the Lord, or upon ethical conceptions which often play their potent part.

To give security to these countless homes, they must be shielded from the two gaunt marauders, war and tyranny. We all know the frightful disturbance in which the ordinary family is plunged when the curse of war swoops down upon the bread-winner and those for whom he works and contrives. The awful ruin of Europe, with all its vanished glories, and of large parts of Asia glares us in the eyes. When the designs of wicked men or the aggressive urge of mighty States dissolve over large areas the frame of civilized society, humble folk are confronted with difficulties with which they cannot cope. For them is all distorted, all is broken, all is even ground to pulp.

When I stand here this quiet afternoon I shudder to visualize what is actually happening to millions now and what is going to happen in this period when famine stalks the earth. None can compute what has been called "the unestimated sum of human pain." Our supreme task and duty is to guard the homes of the common people from the horrors and miseries of another war.

We are all agreed on that.

Our American military colleagues, after having proclaimed their "over-all strategic concept" and computed available resources, always proceed to the next step — namely, the method. Here again there is widespread agreement. A world organization has already been erected for the prime purpose of preventing war. UNO — "U-N-O" — the suc-

Churchill delivering The Sinews of Peace
from www.wikepedia.org

cessor of the League of Nations, with the decisive addition of the United States and all that that means, is already at work. We must make sure that its work is fruitful, that it is a reality and not a sham, that it is a force for action, and not merely a frothing of words, that it is a true temple of peace in which the shields of many nations can some day be hung up, and not merely a cockpit in a Tower of Babel. Before we cast away the solid assurances of national armaments for self-preservation we must be certain that our temple is built, not upon shifting sands or quagmires, but upon the rock. Anyone can see with his — with his eyes open that our path will be difficult and also long, but if we persevere together as we did in the two world wars — though not, alas, in the interval between them — I cannot doubt that we shall achieve our common purpose in the end.

I have, however, a definite and practical proposal to make for action.

Courts and magistrates may be set up but they cannot function without sheriffs and constables. The United Nations Organization must immediately begin to be equipped with an international armed force. In such a matter we can only go step by step, but we must begin now. I propose that each of the Powers and States should be invited to dedicate a certain number of air squadrons to the service of the world organization. These squadrons would be trained and prepared in their own countries, but would move around in rotation from one country to another. They would wear the uniforms of their own countries but with different badges. They would not be required to act against their own nation, but in other respects they would be directed by the world organization. This might be started on a modest scale and it would grow as confidence grew. I wished to see this done after the first world war, and I devoutly trust that it may be done forthwith.

It would nevertheless, ladies and gentlemen, be wrong and imprudent to entrust the secret knowledge or experience of the atomic bomb, which the United States, great Britain, and Canada now share, to the world organization, while it is still in its infancy. It would be criminal madness to cast it adrift in this still agitated and un-united world. No one in any country — No one in any country has slept less well in their beds because this knowledge and the method and the raw materials to apply it, are at present largely retained in American hands. I do not believe we should all have slept so soundly had the positions been reversed and some Communist or neo-Fascist State monopolized for the time being these dread agencies. The fear of them alone might easily have been used to enforce totalitarian systems upon the free democratic world, with consequences appalling to human imagination. God has willed that this shall not be and we have at least a breathing space to set our house in order before this peril has to be encountered. And even then, if no effort is spared, we should still possess so formidable a superiority as to impose effective deterrents upon its employment, or threat of employment, by others. Ultimately, when the essential brotherhood of man is truly embodied and expressed in a world organization with all the necessary practical safeguards to make it effective, these powers would naturally be confided to that world organization.

Now I come to the second of the two marauders, to the second danger which threatens the cottage homes, and ordinary people — namely, tyranny.

We cannot be blind to the fact that the liberties enjoyed by individual citizens throughout the United States and throughout the British Empire are not valid in a considerable number of countries, some of which are very powerful. With these States control is enforced upon the common people by various kinds of all-embracing police governments to a degree which is overwhelming and contrary to every principle of democracy. The power of the State is exercised without restraint, either by dictators or by compact oligarchies operating through a privileged party and a political police. It is not our duty at this time when difficulties are so numerous to interfere forcibly in the internal affairs of countries which we have not conquered in war. But we must never cease to proclaim in fearless tones the great principles of freedom and the rights of man which are the joint inheritance of the English-speaking world and which through Magna Carta, the Bill of Rights, the Habeas Corpus, trial by jury, the English common law find their most famous expression in the American Declaration of Independence.

All this means that the people of any country have the right, and should have the power by constitutional action, by free unfettered elections, with secret ballot, to choose or change the character or form of government under which they dwell; that freedom of speech and thought should reign; that courts of justice, independent of the executive, unbiased by any party, should administer laws which have received the broad assent of large majorities or are consecrated by time and custom. Here are the title deeds of freedom which should lie in every cottage home. Here is the message of the British and American peoples to mankind. Let us preach what we practice — let us practice what we preach.

Though I have now stated the two great dangers which menace the homes of the people, war and tyranny, I have not yet spoken of poverty and privation which are in many cases the prevailing anxiety. But if the dangers of war and tyranny are removed, there is no doubt that science and cooperation can bring in the next few years, certainly in the next few decades, to the world, newly taught in the sharpening school of war, an expansion of material well-being beyond anything that has yet occurred in human experience.

Now, at this sad and breathless moment, we are plunged in the hunger and distress which are the aftermath of our stupendous struggle; but this will pass and may pass quickly, and there is no reason except human folly or sub-human crime which should deny to all the nations the inauguration and enjoyment of an age of plenty. I have often used words which I learned 50 years ago from a great Irish-American orator, a friend of mine, Mr. Bourke Cockran, "There is enough for all. The earth is a generous mother; she will provide in plentiful abundance food for all her children if they will but cultivate her soil in justice and in peace."

And so — So far I — I — I feel that we are in — in full agreement.

Winston Churchill at the Yalta Conference, with Roosevelt and Stanlin beside him (from www.wikipedia.org)

Now, while still pursuing the method — the method of realizing our overall strategic concept, I come to the crux of what I have traveled here to say. Neither the sure prevention of war, nor the continuous rise of world organization will be gained without what I have called the fraternal association of the English-speaking peoples. This means a special relationship between the British Commonwealth and Empire and the United States of America. Ladies and gentlemen, this is no time for generalities, and I will venture to be precise. Fraternal association requires not only the growing friendship and mutual understanding between our two vast but kindred systems of society, but the continuance of the intimate relations between our military advisers, leading to common study of potential dangers, the similarity of weapons and manuals of instruction, and to the interchange of officers and cadets at technical colleges. It should carry with it the continuance of the present facilities for mutual security by the joint use of all Naval and Air Force bases in the possession of either country all over the world. And this — this would perhaps double the mobility of the American Navy and Air Force. It would greatly expand that of the British Empire forces and it might well lead, if and as the world calms down, to important financial savings. Already we use together a large number of islands; more may well be entrusted to our joint care in the near future.

The United States has already a Permanent Defense Agreement with the Dominion of Canada, which is so devotedly attached to the British Commonwealth and Empire. This Agreement is more effective than many of those which have often been made under formal alliances. This principle should be extended to all the British Commonwealths with full reciprocity. Thus, whatever happens, and thus only, shall we be secure ourselves and able to work together for the high and simple causes that are dear to us and bode no ill to any. Eventually — Eventually there may come — I feel eventually there will come — the principle of common citizenship, but that we may be content to leave to destiny, whose outstretched arm many of us can already clearly see.

There is however an important question we must ask ourselves. Would a — a special relationship between the United States and the British Commonwealth be inconsistent with our overriding loyalties to the world organization? I reply that, on the contrary, it is probably the only means by which that organization will achieve its full stature and strength. There are already the special United States relations with Canada which I've just mentioned, and there are the relations between the United States and the South American Republics. We have also — We British have also our twenty years Treaty of Collaboration and Mutual Assistance with Soviet Russia. I agree with Mr. Bevin, the Foreign Secretary of Great Britain, that it might well be a fifty years treaty so far as we are concerned. We aim at nothing but mutual assistance and collaboration with Russia. We have an alliance — The British have an alliance with Portugal unbroken since the year 1384, and which produced fruitful results at a critical moment in the — in the recent war. None of these clash with the general interest of a world agreement, or a world organization; on the contrary, they help it. "In my father's house are many mansions." Special associations between members of the

United Nations which have no aggressive point against any other country, which harbor no design incompatible with the Charter of the United Nations, far from being harmful, are beneficial and, as I believe, indispensable.

I spoke earlier, ladies and gentlemen, of — of the Temple of Peace. Workmen from all countries must build that temple. If two of the workmen know each other particularly well and are old friends, if their families are intermingled, if they have "faith in each other's purpose, hope in each other's future and charity towards each other's shortcomings" — to quote some good words I read here the other day — why cannot they work together at the common task as friends and partners? Why can they not share their tools and thus increase each other's working powers? Indeed they must do so or else the temple may not be built, or, being built, it may collapse, and we should all be proved again unteachable and have to go and try to learn again for a third time in a school of war incomparably more rigorous than that from which we have just been released. The dark ages may return, the Stone Age may return on the gleaming wings of science, and what might now shower immeasurable material blessings upon mankind, may even bring about its total destruction. Beware, I say; time may be short. Do not let us take the course of allowing events to drift along until it is too late. If there is to be a fraternal association of the kind of I have described, with all the express strength and security which both our countries can derive from it, let us make sure that that great fact is known to the world, and that it plays its part in steadying and stabilizing the foundations of peace. There is the path of wisdom. Prevention is better than the cure.

A shadow has fallen upon the scenes so lately light by the Allied victory. Nobody knows what Soviet Russia and its Communist international organization intends to do in the immediate future, or what are the limits, if any, to their expansive and proselytizing tendencies. I have a strong admiration and regard for the valiant Russian people and for my wartime comrade, Marshall Stalin. There — There is deep sympathy and goodwill in Britain — and I doubt not here also — towards the peoples of all the Russias and a resolve to persevere through many differences and rebuffs in establishing lasting friendships. We understand the Russian need to be secure on her western frontiers by the removal of all possibility of German aggression. We welcome Russia to her rightful place among the leading nations of the world. We welcome her flag upon the seas. Above all, we welcome, or should welcome, constant, frequent, and growing contacts between the Russian people and our own peoples on both sides of the Atlantic. It is my duty however, for I am sure you would not wish me to not misstate the... facts as I see them to you. It is my duty to place before you certain facts about the present position in Europe.

From Stettin in the Baltic to Trieste in the Adriatic an iron curtain has descended across the Continent. Behind that line lie all the capitals of the ancient states of Central and Eastern Europe. Warsaw, Berlin, Prague, Vienna, Budapest, Belgrade, Bucharest and Sofia, all these famous cities and the populations around them lie in what I must call the Soviet sphere, and all are subject in one form or another, not only to Soviet influence but to a very high and, in some cases, increasing measure of control from — from Moscow. Athens alone — Greece with its immortal glories — is free to decide its future at an election under British, American, and French observation. The Russian-dominated Polish government has been encouraged to make enormous and wrongful inroads upon Germany, and mass expulsions of millions of Germans on a scale grievous and undreamed-of are now taking place. The Communist parties, which were very small in all these Eastern States of Europe, have been raised to preeminence and power far beyond their numbers and are seeking everywhere to obtain totalitarian control. Police governments are prevailing in nearly every case, and so far, except in Czechoslovakia, there is no true democracy.

Turkey and Persia are both profoundly alarmed and disturbed at the claims which are being made upon them and at the pressure being exerted by the Moscow government. An attempt is being made by the Russians in Berlin to build up a quasi-Communist party in their zone of occupied Germany by showing special favors to groups of left-wing

German leaders. At the end of the fighting last June, the American and British armies withdrew westward, in accordance with an earlier agreement, to a depth at some points of 150 miles upon a front of nearly four hundred miles, in order to allow our Russian allies to occupy this vast expanse of territory which the Western democracies had conquered.

If now the Soviet government tries, by separate action, to build up a pro-Communist Germany in their areas, this will cause new serious difficulties in the American and British zones, and will give the defeated Germans the power of putting themselves up to auction between the Soviets and the Western democracies. Whatever conclusions may be drawn from these facts — and facts they are — this is certainly not the liberated Europe we fought to build up. Nor is it one which contains the essentials of permanent peace.

The safety of the world, ladies and gentlemen, requires a new unity in Europe, from which no nation should be permanently outcast. It is from the quarrels of the strong parent races in Europe that the world wars we have witnessed, or which occurred in former times, have sprung. Twice in our own lifetime we have seen the United States, against their wishes and their traditions, against arguments, the force of which it is impossible — the force of which it is impossible not to comprehend. Twice we have seen them drawn by irresistible forces into these wars in time to secure the victory of the good cause, but only after frightful slaughter and devastation have occurred. Twice the United States has had to send several millions of its young men across the Atlantic to find the war; but now war can find any nation, wherever it may dwell between dusk and dawn. Surely we should work with conscious purpose for a grand pacification of Europe, within the structure of the United Nations and in accordance with our Charter. That, I feel, is — opens a course of policy of very great importance.

In front of the iron curtain which lies across Europe are other causes for anxiety. In Italy the Communist Party is seriously hampered by having to support the Communist-trained Marshal Tito's claims to former Italian territory at the head of the Adriatic. Nevertheless, the future of

Italy hangs in the balance. Again one cannot imagine a regenerated Europe without a strong France. All my public life I worked for a strong France, and I never lost faith in her destiny, even in the darkest hours. I will not lose faith now. However, in a great number of countries, far from the Russian frontiers and throughout the world, Communist fifth columns are established and work in complete unity and absolute obedience to the directions they receive from the Communist center. Except in the British Commonwealth and in the United States where Communism is in its infancy, the Communist parties or fifth columns constitute a growing challenge and peril to Christian civilization. These are somber facts for anyone to have recite on the morrow a victory gained by so much splendid comradeship in arms and in the cause of freedom and democracy; but we should be most unwise not to face them squarely while time remains.

The outlook is also anxious in the Far East and especially in Manchuria. The Agreement which was made at Yalta, to which I was a party, was extremely favorable to Soviet Russia, but it was made at a time when no one could say that the German war might not extend all through the summer and autumn of 1945 and when the Japanese war was expected by the best judges to last for a further 18 months from the end of the German war. In this country you all so well-informed about the Far East, and such devoted friends of China, that I do not need to expatiate on the situation there.

I have, however, felt bound to portray the shadow which, alike in the west and in the east, falls upon the world. I was a minister at the time of the Versailles Treaty and a close friend of Mr. Lloyd-George, who was the head of the British delegation at Versailles. I did not myself agree with many things that were done, but I have a very strong impression in my mind of that situation, and I find it painful to contrast it with that which prevails now. In those days there were high hopes and unbounded confidence that the wars were over and that the League of Nations would become all-powerful. I do not see or feel that same confidence or even the same hopes in the haggard world at the present time.

On the other hand, ladies and gentlemen, I repulse the idea that a new war is inevitable — still more that it is imminent. It is because I am sure that our fortunes are still in our own hands and that we hold the power to save the future, that I feel the duty to speak out now that I have the occasion and the opportunity to do so. I do not believe that Soviet Russia desires war. What they desire is the fruits of war and the indefinite expansion of their power and doctrines. But what we have to consider here today while time remains, is the permanent prevention of war and the establishment of conditions of freedom and democracy as rapidly as possible in all countries. Our difficulties and dangers will not be removed by closing our eyes to them. They will not be removed by mere waiting to see what happens; nor will they be removed by a policy of appeasement. What is needed is a settlement, and the longer this is delayed, the more difficult it will be and the greater our dangers will become.

From what — what I have seen of our Russian friends and Allies during the war, I am convinced that there is nothing they admire so much as strength. And there is nothing for which they have less respect than for weakness, especially military weakness. For that — For that reason the old doctrine of a balance of power is unsound. We cannot afford, if we can help it, to work on narrow margins, offering temptations to a trial of strength. If the Western democracies stand together in strict adherence to the principles of the United Nations Charter there influence for furthering those principles will be immense and no one is likely to molest them. If, however, they become divided or falter in their duty, and if these all-important years are allowed to slip away, then indeed catastrophe may overwhelm us all.

Last time I saw it all coming and I cried aloud to my own fellow countrymen and to the world, but — but no one paid any attention. Up till the year 1933 or even 1935, Germany might have been saved from the awful fate which has overtaken her, and we might all have been spared the miseries Hitler let loose upon mankind. There never was a war in history easier to prevent by timely action than the one which has just desolated such great areas of the globe. It could have been prevented in my belief without the firing of a single shot, and Germany might be powerful, prosperous, and honored today; but no one would listen and one by one we were all sucked into the awful whirlpool. We surely, ladies and gentlemen, I put it to you, surely, we must not let that happen again. This can only be achieved by reaching now, in 1946 — this year, 1946 — by reaching a good understanding on all points with Russia under the general authority of the United Nations Organization and by the maintenance of that good understanding through many peaceful years, by the World Instrument, supported by the whole strength of the English-speaking world and all its connections. There is the solution which I respectfully offer to you in this address to which I have given the title, "The Sinews of Peace."

Let — Let no man underrate the abiding power of the British Empire and — and Commonwealth. Because you see — Because you see the 46 millions in our island harassed about their food supply, of which they only grow one half, even in war-time, or because we have difficulty in restarting our industries and export trade after six years of passionate war effort, do not suppose we shall not come through these dark years of privation as we have come through the glorious years of agony. Do not suppose that half a century from now you will not see 70 or 80 millions of Britons spread about the world united in defense of our traditions, and our way of life, and of the world causes which you and we espouse. If — If the population of the English-speaking Commonwealths be added to that of the United States with all that such cooperation implies in the air, on the sea, all over the globe, and in science, and in industry, and in moral force, there will be no quivering, precarious balance of power to offer its temptation to ambition or adventure. On the contrary, there will be an overwhelming assurance of security. If we adhere faithfully to the Charter of the United Nations and walk forward in sedate and sober strength seeking no one's land or treasure, seeking to lay no arbitrary control upon the thoughts of men; if all British moral and material forces and convictions are joined with your own in fraternal association, the highroads of the future will be clear, not only for us, but for all; not only for our times, but for a century to come.

Words and Expressions Check-Up

sinew *noun* the source of strength, power, or vigor.

recoil *verb* to draw back, start or shrink back, as in alarm, or disgust.

morrow *noun* tomorrow.

accountability *noun* the state of being accountable or liable.

fritter *verb* to dwindle, shrink, degenerate: *to see one's fortune fritter away.*

directive *noun* an authoritative instruction or direction.

privation *noun* the state of being deprived.

gaunt *adjective* extremely thin and bony.

maraud *verb* to raid for plunder.

stalk *verb* to proceed in a steady or deliberate manner: *The drought stalked through the nation.*

sham *noun* something that is not what it purports to be, a spurious imitation.

froth *verb* to cover with froth.

cockpit *noun* a place where a contest is fought or which has been the scene of many contests or battles.

quagmire noun an area of miry or boggy ground whose surface yields under the tread, a bog.

forthwith *adverb* immediately or without delay: *Anyone accused of larceny should be suspended forthwith.*

confide *verb* to entrust, commit to the charge or knowledge of another.

oligarchy *noun* a form of government in which all power is vested in a few persons, government by the few.

menace *noun* something that threatens to cause evil, harm, injury: *Water pollution is a menace to health.*

stupendous *adjective* causing amazement, astounding: *stupendous news.*

crux *noun* a vital, basic, decisive, or pivotal point: *The crux of the trial was his whereabouts at the time.*

proselytize *verb* to convert or attempt to convert as a proselyte.

rebuff *noun* a blunt or abrupt rejection, as of a person making advances.

expulsion *noun* the act of driving out or expelling.

fifth column *noun* a group of people who act traitorously and subversively out of a secret sympathy with an enemy of their country.

squarely *adverb* directly, without evasion, in a straightforward manner.

expatiate *verb* to enlarge in discourse or writing, be copious in description: *to expatiate upon a subject.*

haggard *adjective* having a gaunt, wasted, or exhausted appearance: *thee haggard legs of the tired troops.*

molest *verb* to bother, interfere with, or annoy.

sedate *adjective* calm, quiet, or composed, undisturbed by passion.

Unscramble the words to complete a sentence.

at the pinnacle/ the nation/ world power/ stands/ of

on/ let's/ a modest scale/ start

jewelry/ she/ her sister/ confided/ to

for children/ provide/ she/ will/ food/ all her plentiful

than/ is/ cure/ prevention/ better

differences/ persevere/ we/ through/ resolved/ to/ many

Complete the sentence by filling out the blanks.

그는 새벽같이 일어나는 습관이 있다.

He was ______ ______ rise at dawn.

요즘 여성 가장이 늘어가고 있다.

The number of female _____-______ is increasing these days.

그 기술은 초보단계 수준이다.

The technology is in its _______.

선진국들은 아프리카의 가난에 눈을 감아서는 안 된다.

The advanced countries must not ____ ______ to the poverty problem of Africa.

Georgia는 러시아정부가 가하는 압력 하에 있다.

Georgia is at the pressure being ________ by the Russian government.

문제를 피하지 말고 정면으로 맞서라.

Never avoid, face the problem ________.

문제의 핵심에 도달했다.

We came to the ______ of the matter.

Listen and Fill in the Blanks.

Ladies and gentlemen, the United States stands at this time at the ________ of world power. It is a _______ moment for the American democracy. For with primacy in power is also joined an awe-inspiring __________ to the future. If, as you look around you — If you look around you, you must feel not only the sense of duty done but also you must feel anxiety _______ you ______ _____ the level of achievement. Opportunity is here now, clear and shining for both our countries. To reject it or ignore it or fritter it away will bring upon us all the long __________ of the after-time. It is necessary that constancy of mind, persistency of purpose, and the grand simplicity of decision shall rule and guide the conduct of the English-speaking peoples in _______ as they did in _____r. And we must, and I believe we shall, prove ourselves _______ ____ this severe requirement.

President McCluer, when American military men approach some serious situation they ____ _____ ____ write at the head of their directive the words "over-all strategic concept." There is wisdom in this, as it leads to clarity of thought. What then is the overall strategic concept which we should inscribe today? It is ______ _____ _____ the safety and welfare, the freedom and progress, of all the homes and families of all the men and women in all the lands. And here I speak particularly of the _______ cottage or apartment homes where the _____-______ strives amid the accidents and difficulties of life to guard his wife and children from privation and bring the family up in the fear of the Lord, or upon ethical conceptions which often play their _______part.

To Develop Critical Thinking

In this renowned address, when he coined the term "iron curtain," Winston Churchill proposed that the United Nations should be equipped with military forces and that nuclear weapons should be entrusted to the United Nations as well. Do you agree with this proposal?

Commonwealth of Nations

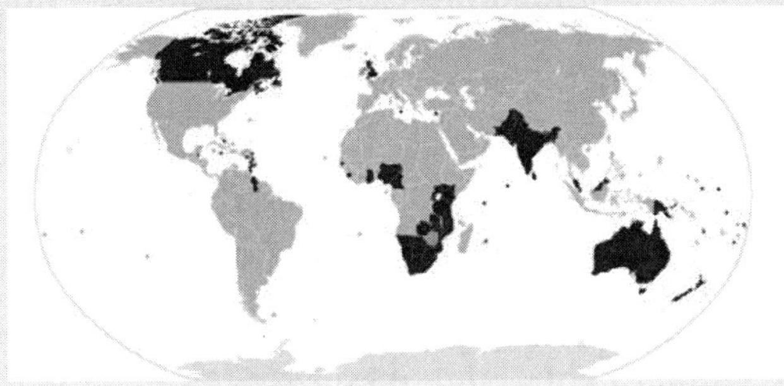

The Commonwealth of Nations, usually known as the Commonwealth, is an intergovernmental organisation of fifty-three independent member states. Most of them were formerly parts of the British Empire. They co-operate within a framework of common values and goals, as outlined in the Singapore Declaration. These include the promotion of democracy, human rights, good governance, the rule of law, individual liberty, egalitarianism, free trade, multilateralism, and world peace. The Commonwealth was established on 11 December 1931. It is not a political union, but an intergovernmental organisation through which countries with diverse social, political, and economic backgrounds are regarded as equal in status. Its activities are carried out through the permanent Commonwealth Secretariat, headed by the Secretary-General; biennial Meetings between Commonwealth Heads of Government; and the Commonwealth Foundation, which facilitates activities of non-governmental organisations in the so-called 'Commonwealth Family'. The symbol of this free association is the Head of the Commonwealth, which is a ceremonial position currently held by Queen Elizabeth II. Elizabeth II is also the monarch, separately, of sixteen members of the Commonwealth, informally called the Commonwealth realms. As each realm is an independent kingdom, the Queen, as monarch, holds a distinct title for each, though, by a Meeting of Commonwealth Prime Ministers in 1952, all include the style *Head of the Commonwealth* at the end; for example: *Elizabeth the Second, by the Grace of God, Queen of Australia and of Her other Realms and Territories, Head of the Commonwealth.* Beyond the realms, the majority of the members of the Commonwealth have separate heads of state: thirty-two members are republics, and five members have distinct monarchs: the Sultan of Brunei; the King of Lesotho; the Yang di-Pertuan Agong (or King) of Malaysia; the King of Swaziland; and the King of Tonga.

The text and image are adopted from www.wikipedia.org

An American Joke: Marine Farmer

One day, Hanson and the Spice Girls were all on an airplane, and they get into a discussion. Baby Spice stated "You know, I could toss a thousand dollars out the window of this plane and make one person very happy." Then, the oldest Hanson brother said, "Well, I could toss ten one hundred dollar bills out the plane and make ten people happy." Then Sporty Spice said, "Well, I could toss one hundred, ten dollar bills out, and make one hundred people happy!" Then the middle Hanson brother very proudly said, "Well, I could toss one thousand, one dollar bills out the window and make one thous and people happy!" Sick of the discussion, another passenger said, "Well, I have a better idea, I could toss all of you out the window and make the entire world happy!"

www.lol-jokes.com/entertainment/music/annoying-pop-stars

Gettysburg Address

delivered on November 19, 1863

by **Abraham Lincoln**

http://www.youtube.com/watch?v=V4bM9geY0do

Four score and seven years ago our fathers brought forth on this continent a new nation, conceived in liberty and dedicated to the proposition that all men are created equal.

The American Civil War (1861–1865) (from www.wikipedia.org)

Now we are engaged in a great civil war, testing whether that nation or any nation so conceived and so dedicated can long endure. We are met on a great battlefield of that war. We have come to dedicate a portion of that field as a final resting-place for those who

The only known photograph of President Lincoln giving his Gettysburg address (from www.wikipedia.org)

here gave their lives that that nation might live. It is altogether fitting and proper that we should do this.

But, in a larger sense, we cannot dedicate, we cannot consecrate, we cannot hallow this ground. The brave men, living and dead who struggled here have consecrated it far above our poor power to add or detract. The world will little note nor long remember what we say here, but it can never forget what they did here. It is for us the living rather to be dedicated here to the unfinished work which they who fought here have thus far so nobly advanced. It is rather for us to be here dedicated to the great task remaining before us — that from these honored dead we take increased devotion to that cause for which they gave the last full measure of devotion — that we here highly resolve that these dead shall not have died in vain, that this nation under God shall have a new birth of freedom, and that government of the people, by the people, for the people shall not perish from the earth.

Union soldiers dead at Gettysburg, photographed by Timothy H. O'Sullivan, July 5-6, 1863 (from www.wikipedia.org)

Words and Expressions Check-Up

consecrate *verb* to make or declare sacred, dedicate to the service of a deity: *to consecrate a new cathedral building.*

detract *verb* to take away a part, as from quality or reputation.

Unscramble the words to complete a sentence.

what/ did/ forget/ the world/ never/ they/ here

all men/ this nation/ to the proposition/ that/ are created/ equal/ dedicated

Complete the sentence by filling out the blanks.

국민의, 국민에 의한, 국민을 위한 정부는 이 땅에서 사라지지 않을 것입니다.

Government ___the people, ___ the people, ___ the people shall not ________ from the earth.

이 죽은 자들은 헛되이 죽지 않을 것입니다.

These dead shall not ______ _______ ____ ________.

To Develop Critical Thinking

The Gettysburg address delivered by Abraham Lincoln is one of the most frequently quoted addresses in US history. However, it is an exceptionally short speech and the words used are simple and plain. Do you like this style of public speech?

An American Joke

As migration approached, two elderly vultures doubted they could make the trip south, so they decided to go by airplane. When they checked their baggage, the attendant noticed that they were carrying two dead raccoons. "Do you wish to check the raccoons through as luggage?" she asked. "No, thanks," replied the vultures. "They're carrion."

www.lol-jokes.com/business-work/aviation/those-raccoons-are-not-luggage

Valedictory Address
to the Labour Party Conference

delivered on 26 September 2006

by **Tony Blair**

http://www.americanrhetoric.com/speeches/tblairfarewell.htm

I'd actually like to start by saying something very simple: Thank you. Thank you to you, our Party, our members, our supporters, the people who week in, week out do the work, take the flak but don't often get the credit. Thank you, the Labour Party for giving me the extraordinary privilege of leading you these past 12 years. Thank you.

I know I look a lot older. That's what being leader of the Labour Party does to you. Actually, looking round some of you look a lot older. That's what having me as leader of the Labour Party does to you. Nobody knows that better, of course, than John Prescott, my deputy these last 12 years, author of "traditional values in a modern setting." I may have taken New Labour to the country; it was you that helped me take it to the Party, so thank you.

And something I don't say often enough — thank you to my family, and to the children, to Cherie [Blair's wife]. I mean — Well, at least I don't have to worry about her running off with the bloke next door. (Sorry, I just couldn't resist that one.)

And it's usual, of course, on the occasions after you thank the family, you thank your agent — and actually I do want to thank my agent John Burton and through him the wonderful people of Sedgefield.

You know, when I went to Sedgefield to seek the nomination, just before the 1983 election, I was a kind of refugee from the London-based politics of the time. And I remember, I knocked on John's door. He said "come in, but shut up for half an hour, we're watching Aberdeen and the Cup Winners' Cup final." And I sat in the company of the most normal people I had met in the Labour Party. And they taught me that most of politics isn't about politics, in the sense of meetings, and resolutions, speeches, even parties sometimes. It starts with people. It's about friendship and art and culture and sport. It's actually about being a fully paid up member of the human race before being a fully paid up member of the Labour Party.

But above all else, I want to thank the British people. Not just for the honor of being Prime Minister but for the journey of progress that we've traveled together. Leaders lead but in the end it's the people who deliver. In the last few months I've seen new hospitals like University College in London, the new Queen Elizabeth Hospital planned in Birmingham — Whiston Hospital in Knowsley, where I laid the foundation stone. But without the talents and dedication of the National Health Service staff, they would be just empty shells. It is their efforts which have cut waiting, improved care, transform and save tens of thousands of lives every day. Thank you.

And we in government, of course, can help put in place the new academy in Liverpool or the ground-breaking Education Village in Darlington, which I've visited recently. But it's the commitment and love of learning of the teachers and their pupils, and the support of parents, which have given our country the best educated children in our history. To them, too, thank you.

And what about this wonderful city of Manchester? A city transformed. A city that shows what a confident, open, and proud people with a great Labour council can do for themselves. So, thank you.

In 1994, I stood before you for the first time, and I shared with you the country's anger at crumbling school buildings, patients languishing, sometimes dying in pain, waiting for operations, of crime doubled, of homes repossessed, of pensioners living in poverty; and I told you of our dismay at four election defeats and how it was not us who should feel betrayed but the British people. That such a speech seems so dated today is not through the passage of time but through progress.

In 1997, we faced daunting challenges: boom and bust economics, chronic under-investment in our public services, social division with millions living in poverty, including over 3 million children at that time. And more than all of that, a country culturally, socially behind. No black ministers — never a black cabinet minister; parliament, supposedly the forum of the people, with only one in 10 women MPs; gay people denied equal rights; trade unionists able to be sacked for joining a trade union; workers on £1.20 an hour, legally; London the only major capital city in the world without city government; Scotland, Wales, Northern Ireland all run from Whitehall; inner cities depleted, a refuge for the dispossessed. This was a country aching for change.

And now, for all that remains to be done, just for a moment dwell on what has been achieved: the longest period of sustained economic growth in British history; mortgage repossession, like mass unemployment, are terms we have to be reminded of; the last NHS winter crisis — six years ago. Heart patients wait on average less than three months; cancer deaths down by 43,000. Today, you are more likely to see a new school building than a crumbling one. There are virtually no long-term unemployed.

Today we ask: Well, can we meet these ambitious targets on child poverty before 1997? The idea of a child poverty target would have been laughable. We have black ministers and the first woman and then the first black woman leader of the Lords. Not enough women MPs but twice what there were. A London mayor, thankfully Labour again. Devolution in Scotland and Wales.

But not just this. Free museum entry that's seen a 50% rise in visitors. Banning things that should never have been allowed: handguns, cosmetic testing on animals; fur farming, blacklisting of trade unionists and from summer next year, smoking in public places. And allowing things that should never have been banned: the right to roam; the right to request flexible working; civil partnerships for gay people. And in 2012 it is London that will host the Olympic games. Of course, the daily coverage of politics focuses on the negative. But take a step back and be proud. This is a changed country. Above all, it is progressive ideas which define its politics. That's the real result of a third term victory.

And there's the Tories having to pretend they love it all: Bank of England independence, they never did in 18 years; the minimum wage, they told us would cost a million jobs; help for the world's poor that they cut. Now, they fall over themselves saying how much they agree with us. Don't lose heart from that; take heart from it.

We've changed the terms of political debate. This Labour government has been unique. First time ever two full terms; now three. So, why? And how? Because we faced out to the people, not in on ourselves. We put the Party at the service of the country. Their reality became our reality. Their worries, our worries. We abandoned the ridiculous, self-imposed dilemma between principle and power. We went back to first principles, our values, our real values, those that are timeless, and separated them from doctrine and dogma that had been ravaged by time.

And in doing so, we freed Britain at long last from the reactionary choice that dominated British politics for so long: between individual prosperity and a caring society. We proved that economic efficiency and social justice are not opposites but partners in progress. We defied conventional political wisdom and thereby we changed it. And around that we built a new political coalition.

The USP of New Labour is aspiration and compassion reconciled. We reach out not just to those in poverty or need but those who are doing well but want to do better; those on their way up, ambitious for themselves and their families. These are our people too, not to be tolerated for electoral reasons but embraced out of political conviction. The core vote of this Party today is not the heartlands, the inner city, not any sectional interest or lobby. Our core vote is the country. And it was they who made us change.

The beliefs of the Labour Party of 2006 should be recognizable to the members of 1906. And they are: full employment, strong public services, tackling poverty, international solidarity. But the policies shouldn't. And the trouble was for a long time they were. In the 1960s, re-reading the cabinet debates of In Place of Strife, everyone was telling Harold Wilson not to push it. It was divisive, unnecessary, alienated core support. And in the end he gave up but so did the public on Labour. Even in 1974, the Labour government spent two years renationalizing shipbuilding and the public spent two years wondering why. In the 1980s, council house sales had first been suggested by Labour people. It was shelved. Too difficult. Too divisive. And we lost a generation of aspiring working class people on the back of it. In the 1980s we should have been the Party transforming Britain. But we weren't.

And the lesson is always the same. Values unrelated to modern reality are not just electorally hopeless, the values themselves become devalued. They have no purchase on the real world. We won in the end not because we surrendered our values but because we finally had the courage to be true to them. And our courage, then, in changing gave the British people the courage to change. That's how we won.

And 10 years after, government takes its toll. It does. It's in the nature of the beast. And in the harsh climate of the 24/7 media, in which gossip and controversy are so much more newsworthy than real news, people forget. I spoke to a woman the other day, a part-time worker, complaining about the amount of her tax credit. And I said, hold on a minute: before 1997, there were no tax credits, not for working families, not for any families; child benefit was frozen; maternity pay half what it is; maternity leave likewise; paternity leave didn't exist at all; no minimum wage; no full time rights for part time workers; in fact, nothing. "So what?", she said, "That's why we elected you. Now go and sort out my tax credit."

And, of course, she's right. In government you — you carry each hope, each disillusion. And in politics it's always about the next challenge. The truth is, you can't go on forever. That's why it's right that this is my last conference as Leader. And of course it's hard to let go. But it's also right to let go — for the country, and for you, the Party.

And over the coming months, I will take through the changes I've worked on so hard these past years. And I'll try to help build a unified Party with a strong platform for the only legacy that has ever mattered to me — a fourth term election victory that allows us to keep on changing Britain for the better.

And I want to heal. There's been a lot of talk of lies and truths these past few weeks. In any relationship at the top of any walk of life it isn't always easy, least of all in politics which matters so much and which is conducted in such a piercing spotlight. But I know New Labour would never have happened, and three election victories would never have been secured, without Gordon Brown. He's a remarkable man, a remarkable servant to this country, and that is the truth.

Words and Expressions Check-Up

valedictory *adjective* bidding good-bye, saying farewell: *a valedictory speech.*

flak *noun* excessive or abusive criticism.

bloke *noun* British Informal. man, fellow, guy.

* **Sedgefield** A small town in County Durham, England. It has a population of approximately 5,000. Sedgefield is in the parish of Upper Skerne. Sedgefield has attracted particular attention as the Member of Parliament for the wider Sedgefield constituency was the former Prime Minister Tony Blair. (www.wikipedia.org)

sack *verb* Slang to dismiss or discharge, as from a job.

* **Whitehall** Whitehall is a road in Westminster in London, England. It is the main artery running north from Parliament Square, towards traditional Charing Cross, now at the southern end of Trafalgar Square and marked by the statue of Charles I, which is often regarded as the heart of London. Recognised as centre of HM Government, the road is lined with government departments/ministries; "Whitehall" is therefore also frequently used as a metonym for governmental administration, as well as being a geographic name for the surrounding district tax credit. (www.wikipedia.org)

NHS = National Health Service

devolution *noun* the transfer of power or authority from a central government to a local government.

fall all over oneself *idiom* to show unusual or excessive enthusiasm or eagerness in the hope of being favored or rewarded.

ravage *verb* to work havoc upon, damage by ravages.

at long last *idiom* after much troublesome or frustrating delay: *They arrived at long last.*

tax credit *noun* A dollar-for-dollar reduction in the tax payment required from a person.

sort out *idiom* to put in order, clarify: *After I sort things out there, I'll be able to concentrate on my study.*

maternity leave *noun* a leave of absence for an expectant or new mother for the birth and care of the baby.

24/7 continually, constantly: *The couple is together 24/7.*

Unscramble the words to complete a sentence.

older/ know/ I/ a lot/ I look

was/ just/ an empty shell/ the building

I/ the people's/ you/ with/ anger/ share

flexible/ we/ working/ need/ hours

we/ reality/ is/ their reality/ our/ realized

efficiency/ opposites/ justice/ and/ are not.

we surrendered/ we won/ not because/ our values

Complete the sentence by filling out the blanks.

매주 빠짐없이 교회에 가는 것이 필요하다.

It is necessary to go to church ______ ___, ______ ____.

누구나 자신이 한 일에 대해 공을 인정받고 싶어 한다.

Everybody wants to ______ the ______for what he did.

그의 들쭉날쭉한 성격 때문에 걱정이다.

We are concerned about his _______ and (or) _______ character.

정치에 대한 최근 보도는 부정적인 면에 집중된다.

The daily _____ of politics focuses on the ________.

그 일로부터 용기를 잃지 말고 용기를 얻어라.

Don't _______ _____ from that but _______ ______ from it.

천신만고 끝에 그 일을 해냈다.

____ ____ _____ we finished the job.

Listen and Fill in the Blanks.

But above all else, I want to thank the British people. Not just for the _____ of being Prime Minister but for the journey of progress that we've ______ _______. Leaders lead but in the end it's the people who ______. In the last few months I've seen new hospitals like University College in London, the new Queen Elizabeth Hospital planned in Birmingham — Whiston Hospital in Knowsley, where I laid the foundation stone. But without the ______ and ________ of the National Health Service staff, they would be just ______ ______. It is their efforts which have _____ waiting, improved care, transform and save tens of thousands of lives every day. Thank you. And we in government, of course, can help put ____ _____ the new academy in Liverpool or the ground-breaking Education Village in Darlington, which I've visited recently. But it's the _________ and love of learning of the teachers and their pupils, and the support of parents, which have given our country the best educated children in our history. To them, too, thank you.

And what about this wonderful city of Manchester? A city transformed. A city that shows what a confident, open, and proud people with a great Labour council can do for themselves. So, thank you.

In 1994, I stood before you for the first time, and I ______ with you the country's anger at _______ school buildings, patients ________, sometimes dying in pain, waiting for operations, of crime doubled, of homes repossessed, of pensioners living in poverty; and I told you of our _______ at four election defeats and how it was not us who should feel _______ but the British people. That such a speech seems so _____ today is not through the passage of time but through progress.

To Develop Critical Thinking

Tony Blair is recognized as one of the greatest prime ministers in the UK. In his farewell address to the Labour Party, he listed what his administration achieved during the past twelve years. Do you think he deserves to be praised as a prime minister?

Labour Party (UK)

The Labour Party is a centre-left/centrist political party and current ruling party in the United Kingdom. Founded at the start of the 20th century, it has been since the 1920s the principal party of the left in England, Scotland and Wales, but not Northern Ireland, where it has only recently organised again. Under New Labour, the party's position moved towards the centre. Labour surpassed the Liberal Party as the main opposition to the Conservatives in the early 1920s. It has had several spells in government, first as minority governments under Ramsay MacDonald in 1924 and 1929~31, then as a junior partner in the wartime coalition from 1940-1945, and then as a majority government, under Clement Attlee in 1945~51 and under Harold Wilson in 1964~70. Labour was in government again in 1974-79, under Wilson and then James Callaghan, though with a precarious and declining majority.

www.wikipedia.org

A British Joke

One day a boy asks "Where's your bathroom?"

"Right in the left back corner of the store," the manager said. So he walks into the bathroom and noticed there was no toilet, just a bath. So he comes out and says "What gives, There is no toilet in the bathroom."

"Duh," said the manager, "you didn't ask for a toilet room, you asked for a bathroom"!

http:www.thejokes.co.uk/british-humour.php

Epoch-Making Speeches

The Lady's Not for Turning

Speech to Conservative Party Conference

delivered on 10 October, 1980

by **Margaret Thatcher**

http://www.youtube.com/watch?v=rQ-M0KEFm9I

Mr chairman, ladies and gentlemen, most of my Cabinet colleagues have started their speeches of reply by paying very well deserved tributes to their junior Ministers. At Number 10 I have no junior Ministers. There is just [Denis Thatcher] Denis and me, and I could not do without him.

I am, however, very fortunate in having a marvellous deputy who is wonderful in all places at all times in all things — Willie Whitelaw.

At our party conference last year I said that the task in which the Government were engaged — to change the national attitude of mind — was the most challenging to face any British Administration since the war. Challenge is exhilarating. This week we Conservatives have been taking stock, discussing the achievements, the set-backs and the work that lies ahead as we enter our second parliamentary year. As you said Mr Chairman our debates have been stimulating and our debates have been constructive. This week has demonstrated that we are a party united in purpose, strategy and resolve. And we actually like one another.

Falkland war and Margaret Thatcher
(from www.wikipedia.org)

When I am asked for a detailed forecast of what will happen in the coming months or years I remember Sam Goldwyn's advice: "Never prophesy, especially about the future." (Interruption from the floor) Never mind, it is wet outside. I expect that they wanted to come in. You cannot blame them; it is always better where the Tories are. And you — and perhaps they — will be looking to me this afternoon for an indication of how the Government see the task before us and why we are tackling it the way we are. Before I begin let me get one thing out of the way.

This week at Brighton we have heard a good deal about last week at Blackpool. I will have a little more to say about that strange assembly later, but for the moment I want to say just this.

Because of what happened at that conference, there has been, behind all our deliberations this week, a heightened awareness that now, more than ever, our Conservative Government must succeed. We just must, because now there is even more at stake than some had realised.

There are many things to be done to set this nation on the road to recovery, and I do not mean economic recovery alone, but a new independence of spirit and zest for achievement.

It is sometimes said that because of our past we, as a people, expect

Thatcher delivering Speech to Conservative Party Conference in 1980 (from www.wikipedia.org)

too much and set our sights too high. That is not the way I see it. Rather it seems to me that throughout my life in politics our ambitions have steadily shrunk. Our response to disappointment has not been to lengthen our stride but to shorten the distance to be covered. But with confidence in ourselves and in our future what a nation we could be!

In its first seventeen months this Government have laid the foundations for recovery. We have undertaken a heavy load of legislation, a load we do not intend to repeat because we do not share the Socialist fantasy that achievement is measured by the number of laws you pass. But there was a formidable barricade of obstacles that we had to sweep aside. For a start, in his first Budget Geoffrey Howe began to rest incentives to stimulate the abilities and inventive genius of our people. Presperity comes not from grand conferences of economists but by countless acts of personal self-confidence and self-reliance.

Under Geoffrey 's stewardship, Britain has repaid $3,600 million of international debt, debt which had been run up by our predecessors. And we paid quite a lot of it before it was due. In the past twelve months Geoffrey has abolished exchange controls over which British Governments have dithered for decades. Our great enterprises are now free to seek opportunities overseas. This will help to secure our living standards long after North Sea oil has run out. This Government thinks about the future. We have made the first crucial changes in trade union law to remove the worst abuses of the closed shop, to restrict picketing to the place of work of the parties in dispute, and to encourage secret ballots.

Jim Prior has carried all these measures through with the support of the vast majority of trade union members. Keith Joseph, David Howell, John Nott and Norman Fowler have begun to break down the monopoly powers of nationalisation. Thanks to them British Aerospace will soon be open to private investment. The monopoly of the Post Office and British Telecommunications is being diminished. The barriers to private generation of electricity for sale have been lifted. For the first time nationalised industries and public utilities can be investigated by the Monopolies Commission — a long overdue reform.

Free competition in road passenger transport promises travellers a better deal. Michael Heseltine has given to millions — yes, millions — of council tenants the right to buy their own homes.

It was Anthony Eden who chose for us the goal of "a property-owning democracy". But for all the time that I have been in public affairs that has been beyond the reach of so many, who were denied the right to the most basic ownership of all — the homes in which they live.

They wanted to buy. Many could afford to buy. But they happened to live under the jurisdiction of a Socialist council, which would not sell and did not believe in the independence that comes with ownership. Now Michael Heseltine has given them the chance to turn a dream into reality. And all this and a lot more in seventeen months.

The Left continues to refer with relish to the death of capitalism. Well, if this is the death of capitalism, I must say that it is quite a way to go.

But all this will avail us little unless we achieve our prime economic objective — the defeat of inflation. Inflation destroys nations and societies as surely as invading armies do. Inflation is the parent of unemployment. It is the unseen robber of those who have saved.

No policy which puts at risk the defeat of inflation — however great its short-term attraction — can be right. Our policy for the defeat of inflation is, in fact, traditional. It existed long before Sterling M3 embellished the Bank of England Quarterly Bulletin, or "monetarism" became a convenient term of political invective.

But some people talk as if control of the money supply was a revolutionary policy. Yet it was an essential condition for the recovery of much of continental Europe.

Those countries knew what was required for economic stability. Previously, they had lived through rampant inflation; they knew that it led to suitcase money, massive unemployment and the breakdown of society itself. They determined never to go that way again.

Today, after many years of monetary self-discipline, they have stable, prosperous economies better able than ours to withstand the buffeting of world recession.

So at international conferences to discuss economic affairs many of my fellow Heads of Government find our policies not strange, unusual or revolutionary, but normal, sound and honest. And that is what they are.

Their only question is: "Has Britain the courage and resolve to sustain the discipline for long enough to break through to success?"

Yes, Mr. Chairman, we have, and we shall. This Government are determined to stay with the policy and see it through to its conclusion. That is what marks this administration as one of the truly radical ministries of post-war Britain. Inflation is falling and should continue to fall.

Meanwhile we are not heedless of the hardships and worries that accompany the conquest of inflation.

Foremost among these is unemployment. Today our country has more than 2 million unemployed.

Now you can try to soften that figure in a dozen ways. You can point out—and it is quite legitimate to do so — that 2 million today does not mean what it meant in the 1930s; that the percentage of unemployment is much less now than it was then.

You can add that today many more married women go out to work.

You can stress that, because of the high birthrate in the early 1960s, there is an unusually large number of school leavers this year looking for work and that the same will be true for the next two years.

You can emphasise that about a quarter of a million people find new jobs each month and therefore go off the employment register.

And you can recall that there are nearly 25 million people in jobs compared with only about 18 million in the 1930s. You can point out that the Labour party conveniently overlooks the fact that of the 2 million unemployed for which they blame us, nearly a million and a half were bequeathed by their Government.

But when all that has been said the fact remains that the level of unemployment in our country today is a human tragedy. Let me make it clear beyond doubt. I am profoundly concerned about unemployment. Human dignity and self respect are undermined when men and women are condemned to idleness. The waste of a country's most precious assets — the talent and energy of its people- makes it the bounden duty of Government to seek a real and lasting cure.

If I could press a button and genuinely solve the unemployment problem, do you think that I would not press that button this instant? Does anyone imagine that there is the smallest political gain in letting this unemployment continue, or that there is some obscure economic religion which demands this unemployment as part of its ritual? This Government are pursuing the only policy which gives any hope of bringing our people back to real and lasting employment. It is no coincidence that those countries, of which I spoke earlier, which have had lower rates of inflation have also had lower levels of unemployment.

I know that there is another real worry affecting many of our people. Although they accept that our policies are right, they feel deeply that the burden of carrying them out is falling much more heavily on the private than on the public sector. They say that the public sector is enjoying advantages but the private sector is taking the knocks and at the same time maintaining those in the public sector with better pay and pensions than they enjoy.

I must tell you that I share this concern and understand the resentment. That is why I and my colleagues say that to add to public spending takes away the very money and resources that industry needs to stay in business let alone to expand. Higher public spending, far from curing unemployment, can be the very vehicle that loses jobs and causes bankruptcies in trade and commerce. That is why we warned local authorities that since rates are frequently the biggest tax that industry now faces, increases in them can cripple local businesses. Councils must, therefore, learn to cut costs in the same way that companies have to.

That is why I stress that if those who work in public authorities take for themselves large pay increases they leave less to be spent on equipment and new buildings. That in turn deprives the private sector of the orders it needs, especially some of those industries in the hard pressed regions. Those in the public sector have a duty to those in the private sector not to take out so much in pay that they cause others unemployment. That is why we point out that every time high wage settlements in nationalised monopolies lead to higher charges for telephones, electricity, coal and water, they can drive companies out of business and cost other people their jobs.

If spending money like water was the answer to our country's problems, we would have no problems now. If ever a nation has spent, spent, spent and spent again, ours has. Today that dream is over. All of that money has got us nowhere but it still has to come from somewhere. Those who urge us to relax the squeeze, to spend yet more money indiscriminately in the belief that it will help the unemployed and the small businessman are not being kind or compassionate or caring.

They are not the friends of the unemployed or the small business. They are asking us to do again the very thing that caused the problems in the first place. We have made this point repeatedly.

I am accused of lecturing or preaching about this. I suppose it is a critic's way of saying "Well, we know it is true, but we have to carp at something." I do not care about that. But I do care about the future of free enterprise, the jobs and exports it provides and the independence it brings to our people. Independence? Yes, but let us be clear what we mean by that. Independence does not mean contracting out of all relationships with others. A nation can be free but it will not stay free for long if it has no friends and no alliances. Above all, it will not stay free if it cannot pay its own way in the world. By the same token, an individual needs to be part of a community and to feel that he is part of it. There is more to this than the chance to earn a living for himself and his family, essential though that is.

Of course, our vision and our aims go far beyond the complex arguments of economics, but unless we get the economy right we shall deny our people the opportunity to share that vision and to see beyond the narrow horizons of economic necessity. Without a healthy economy we cannot have a healthy society. Without a healthy society the economy will not stay healthy for long.

But it is not the State that creates a healthy society. When the State grows too powerful people feel that they count for less and less. The State drains society, not only of its wealth but of initiative, of energy, the will to improve and innovate as well as to preserve what is best. Our aim is to let people feel that they count for more and more. If we cannot trust the deepest instincts of our people we should not be in politics at all. Some aspects of our present society really do offend those instincts.

Decent people do want to do a proper job at work, not to be restrained or intimidated from giving value for money. They believe that honesty should be respected, not derided. They see crime and violence as a threat not just to society but to their own orderly way of life. They want to be allowed to bring up their children in these beliefs, without the fear that their efforts will be daily frustrated in the name of progress or free expression. Indeed, that is what family life is all about.

There is not a generation gap in a happy and united family. People yearn to be able to rely on some generally accepted standards. Without them you have not got a society at all, you have purposeless anarchy. A healthy society is not created by its institutions, either. Great schools and universities do not make a great nation any more than great armies do. Only a great nation can create and involve great institutions — of learning, of healing, of scientific advance. And a great nation is the voluntary creation of its people — a people composed of men and women whose pride in themselves is founded on the knowledge of what they can give to a community of which they in turn can be proud.

If our people feel that they are part of a great nation and they are prepared to will the means to keep it great, a great nation we shall be, and shall remain. So, what can stop us from achieving this? What then stands in our way? The prospect of another winter of discontent? I suppose it might.

But I prefer to believe that certain lessons have been learnt from experience, that we are coming, slowly, painfully, to an autumn of understanding. And I hope that it will be followed by a winter of common sense. If it is not, we shall not be — diverted from our course.

To those waiting with bated breath for that favourite media catchphrase, the "U" turn, I have only one thing to say. "You turn if you want to. The lady's not for turning." I say that not only to you but to our friends overseas and also to those who are not our friends.

In foreign affairs we have pursued our national interest robustly while remaining alive to the needs and interests of others. We have acted where our predecessors dithered and here I pay tribute to Lord Carrington. When I think of our much-travelled Foreign Secretary I am reminded of the advert, you know the one I mean, about "The peer that reaches those foreign parts that other peers cannot reach."

Long before we came into office, and therefore long before the invasion of Afghanistan I was pointing to the threat from the East. I was accused of scaremongering. But events have more than justified my words.

Soviet Marxism is ideologically, politically and morally bankrupt. But militarily the Soviet Union is a powerful and growing threat.

Yet it was Mr. Kosygin who said "No peace loving country, no person of integrity, should remain indifferent when an aggressor holds human life and world opinion in insolent contempt." We agree. The British Government are not indifferent to the occupation of Afghanistan. We shall not allow it to be forgotten. Unless and until the Soviet troops are withdrawn other nations are bound to wonder which of them may be next. Of course there are those who say that by speaking out we are complicating East-West relations, that we are endangering detente. But the real danger would lie in keeping silent. Detente is indivisible and it is a two-way process.

The Soviet Union cannot conduct wars by proxy in South-East Asia and Africa, foment trouble in the Middle East and Caribbean and invade neighbouring countries and still expect to conduct business as usual. Unless detente is pursued by both sides it can be pursued by neither, and it is a delusion to suppose otherwise. That is the message we shall be delivering loud and clear at the meeting of the European Security Conference in Madrid in the weeks immediately ahead.

But we shall also be reminding the other parties in Madrid that the Helsinki Accord was supposed to promote the freer movement of people and ideas. The Soviet Government's response so far has been a campaign of repression worse than any since Stalin 's day. It had been hoped that Helsinki would open gates across Europe. In fact, the guards today are better armed and the walls are no lower. But behind those walls the human spirit is unvanquished.

The workers of Poland in their millions have signalled their determination to participate in the shaping of their destiny. We salute them.

Marxists claim that the capitalist system is in crisis. But the Polish workers have shown that it is the Communist system that is in crisis. The Polish people should be left to work out their own future without external interference.

At every Party Conference, and every November in Parliament, we used to face difficult decisions over Rhodesia and over sanctions. But no longer. Since we last met the success at Lancaster House, and thereafter in Salisbury — a success won in the face of all the odds — has created new respect for Britain. It has given fresh hope to those grappling with the terrible problems of Southern Africa. It has given the Commonwealth new strength and unity. Now it is for the new nation, Zimbabwe, to build her own future with the support of all those who believe that democracy has a place in Africa, and we wish her well.

We showed over Rhodesia that the hallmarks of Tory policy are, as they have always been, realism and resolve. Not for us the disastrous fantasies of unilateral disarmament, of withdrawal from NATO, of abandoning Northern Ireland.

The irresponsibility of the Left on defence increases as the dangers which we face loom larger. We for our part, under Francis Pym 's brilliant leadership, have chosen a defence policy which potential foes will respect.

We are acquiring, with the co-operation of the United States Government, the Trident missile system. This will ensure the credibility of our strategic deterrent until the end of the century and beyond, and it was very important for the reputation of Britain abroad that we should keep our independent nuclear deterrent as well as for our citizens here.

We have agreed to the stationing of Cruise missiles in this country. The unilateralists object, but the recent willingness of the Soviet Government to open a new round of arms control negotiations shows the wisdom of our firmness.

We intend to maintain and, where possible, to improve our conventional forces so as to pull our weight in the Alliance. We have no wish to seek a free ride at the expense of our Allies. We will play our full part.

In Europe we have shown that it is possible to combine a vigorous defence of our own interests with a deep commitment to the idea and to the ideals of the Community.

The last Government were well aware that Britain's budget contribution was grossly unfair. They failed to do anything about it. We negotiated a satisfactory arrangement which will give us and our partners time to tackle the underlying issues. We have resolved the difficulties of New Zealand's lamb trade with the Community in a way which protects the interests of the farmers in New Zealand while giving our own farmers and our own housewives an excellent deal, and Peter Walker deserves to be congratulated on his success. Now he is two-thirds on his way to success in making important progress towards agreement on a common fisheries policy. That is very important to our people. There are many, many people whose livelihoods depend on it.

We face many other problems in the Community, but I am confident that they too will yield to the firm yet fair approach which has already proved so much more effective than the previous Government's five years of procrastination.

With each day it becomes clearer that in the wider world we face darkening horizons, and the war between Iran and Iraq is the latest symptom of a deeper malady. Europe and North America are centres of stability in an increasingly anxious world. The Community and the Alliance are the guarantee to other countries that democracy and freedom of choice are still possible. They stand for order and the rule of law in an age when disorder and lawlessness are ever more widespread.

The British Government intend to stand by both these great institutions, the Community and NATO. We will not betray them.

The restoration of Britain's place in the world and of the West's confidence in its own destiny are two aspects of the same process. No doubt there will be unexpected twists in the road, but with wisdom and resolution we can reach our goal. I believe we will show the wisdom and you may be certain that we will show the resolution.

In his warm hearted and generous speech, Peter Thorneycroft said that, when people are called upon to lead great nations they must look into the hearts and minds of the people whom they seek to govern. I would add that those who seek to govern must in turn be willing to allow their hearts and minds to lie open to the people.

This afternoon I have tried to set before you some of my most deeply held convictions and beliefs. This Party, which I am privileged to serve, and this Government, which I am proud to lead, are engaged in the massive task of restoring confidence and stability to our people.

I have always known that that task was vital. Since last week it has become even more vital than ever. We close our Conference in the aftermath of that sinister Utopia unveiled at Blackpool. Let Labour's Orwellian nightmare of the Left be the spur for us to dedicate with a new urgency our every ounce of energy and moral strength to rebuild the fortunes of this free nation.

If we were to fail, that freedom could be imperilled. So let us resist the blandishments of the faint hearts; let us ignore the howls and threats of the extremists; let us stand together and do our duty, and we shall not fail.

Words and Expressions Check-Up

take stock *idiom* to make an appraisal of resources or prospects.

set-back *noun* a check to progress, a reverse or defeat: *The new rule was a setback.*

dither *verb* to act irresolutely, vacillate.

buffet *verb* to strike against or push repeatedly: *The snowstorm buffeted the house.*

bounden *adjective* obligatory, compulsory: *one's bounden responsibility.*

carp *verb* to find fault or complain querulously: *to carp a trivial errors.*

by the same token *idiom* moreover, furthermore: *She has a talent as a painter, and by the same token has a sharp eye for music.*

advert = advertisement

scaremonger *noun* a person who creates or spreads alarming news.

foment *verb* to instigate or foster discord, rebellion, promote the growth or development of.

grossly *adverb* completely.

procrastinate *verb* to defer action, delay: *to procrastinate until the chance is lost.*

blandish *verb* to coax or influence by gentle flattery, cajole: *He blandished the security into letting him through the gate.*

Unscramble the words to complete a sentence.

too much/ don't expect/ and/ high/ our goals/ too/ set

this government/ recovery/ laid/ for/ the foundation

in/ affairs/ was/ his life/ successful/ public

afford/ to/ people/ could/ many/ buy

the parent/ inflation/ of/ unemployment/ is

married/ go out/ today/ many/ women/ to work

carp/ we/ the mayor/ have/ to/ at

Complete the sentence by filling out the blanks.

재고조사를 하고 나서 바꾸기로 했다.

She _____ ______ of items and decided it was time for a change.

비밀투표는 장려되어야 한다.

Secret ballots should be _________.

국영기업체와 공공시설들이 조사를 받았다.

__________ industries and ________ utilities were investigated.

때늦은 개혁은 실효성이 없을 가능성이 있다.

The ________ reform is not going to be effective.

그 정치가는 꿈을 현실로 만들었다.

The politician _____ a dream _____ _______.

우리는 끝장을 보고야 말겠습니다.

We want to _____ it _______ to its conclusion.

그 가게는 망했다.

The shop is _____ ____ business.

Listen and Fill in the Blanks.

In its first seventeen months this Government has ______ the foundations for _______. We have undertaken a heavy load of legislation, a load we do not intend to repeat because we do not ______ the Socialist ______ that achievement is measured by the number of laws you pass. But there was a formidable barricade of obstacles that we had to sweep aside. For a start, in his first Budget Geoffrey Howe began to rest incentives to stimulate the abilities and inventive genius of our people. ________ ______ not from grand conferences of economists but by countless acts of personal self-confidence and self-reliance.
Under Geoffrey's stewardship, Britain has repaid $3,600 million of international debt, debt which had been _____ ______ by our predecessors. And we paid quite a lot of it before it was ______. In the past twelve months Geoffrey has abolished exchange controls over which British Governments have ________ for decades. Our great enterprises are now free to seek opportunities overseas. This will help to secure our living standards long after North Sea oil has ____ _____. This Government thinks about the future. We have made the first crucial changes in trade union law to remove the worst abuses of the closed shop, to restrict picketing to the place of work of the parties in dispute, and to ________ secret ballots.
Jim Prior has carried all these measures through with the support of the vast majority of trade union members. Keith Joseph, David Howell, John Nott and Norman Fowler have begun to ______ ______ the monopoly powers of ___________. Thanks to them British Aerospace will soon be open to private investment. The monopoly of the Post Office and British Telecommunications

is being ________. The barriers to private generation of electricity for sale have been lifted. For the first time nationalised industries and public utilities can be investigated by the Monopolies Commission — a long ______ reform.

To Develop Critical Thinking

For a veteran politician, Margaret Thatcher's message to be conveyed to the audience is pretty clear and obvious. In this sense, her speech seems to defy our conventional concept of a "politician," which tends to have a negative connotation. What do you think about Margaret Thatcher as a politician?

An American Joke

What is the difference between a Canadian fairy tale and Alabama fairy tale?

Canadian fairy tales start with — once upon a time, Alabama fairy tales start with — yo, yall ain't gonna believe this.

www.lol-jokes.com/entertainment/other/fairy-tales

Epoch-Making Speeches

Pearl Harbor Address to the Nation

delivered on December 8, 1941

by **Franklin Delano Roosevelt**

http://www.americanrhetoric.com/speeches/fdrpearlharbor.htm

Mr. Vice President, Mr. Speaker, Members of the Senate, and of the House of Representatives:

Yesterday, December 7th, 1941 — a date which will live in infamy — the United States of America was suddenly and deliberately attacked by naval and air forces of the Empire of Japan.

The United States was at peace with that nation and, at the solicitation of Japan, was still in conversation with its government and its emperor looking toward the maintenance of peace in the Pacific.

Indeed, one hour after Japanese air squadrons had commenced bombing in the American island of Oahu, the Japanese ambassador to the

Pearl Harbor Address to the Nation

United States and his colleague delivered to our Secretary of State a formal reply to a recent American message. And while this reply stated that it seemed useless to continue the existing diplomatic negotiations, it contained no threat or hint of war or of armed attack.

It will be recorded that the distance of Hawaii from Japan makes it obvious that the attack was deliberately planned many days or even weeks ago. During the intervening time, the Japanese government has deliberately sought to deceive the United States by false statements and expressions of hope for continued peace.

The attack yesterday on the Hawaiian islands has caused severe damage to American naval and military forces. I regret to tell you that very many American lives have been lost. In addition, American ships have been reported torpedoed on the high seas between San Francisco and Honolulu.

Yesterday, the Japanese government also launched an attack against Malaya.

Last night, Japanese forces attacked Hong Kong.

Last night, Japanese forces attacked Guam.

Last night, Japanese forces attacked the Philippine Islands.

Last night, the Japanese attacked Wake Island.

And this morning, the Japanese attacked Midway Island.

Japan has, therefore, undertaken a surprise offensive extending throughout the Pacific area. The facts of yesterday and today speak for themselves. The people of the United States have already formed their opinions and well understand the implications to the very life and safety of our nation.

As commander in chief of the Army and Navy, I have directed that all measures be taken for our defense. But always will our whole nation remember the character of the onslaught against us.

No matter how long it may take us to overcome this premeditated invasion, the American people in their righteous might will win through to absolute victory.

I believe that I interpret the will of the Congress and of the people when I assert that we will not only defend ourselves to the uttermost, but will make it very certain that this form of treachery shall never again endanger us.

Hostilities exist. There is no blinking at the fact that our people, our territory, and our interests are in grave danger.

With confidence in our armed forces, with the unbounding determination of our people, we will gain the inevitable triumph — so help us God.

I ask that the Congress declare that since the unprovoked and dastardly attack by Japan on Sunday, December 7th, 1941, a state of war has existed between the United States and the Japanese empire.

Words and Expressions Check-Up

infamy *noun* extremely bad reputation, public reproach, as the result of a shameful, criminal act.

soliciatation *noun* urging, a petition or request.

blink *verb* to look evasively or indifferently, ignore.

dastard *noun* a mean, sneaking coward.

Unscramble the words to complete a sentence.

been lost/ many/ lives/ have/ Korean War/ by

on the high seas / attacked / the battle ships/ were

Complete the sentence by filling out the blanks.

지난 태풍은 막대한 손실을 끼쳤다.

The last rainstorm _______ enormous _______ to us.

일본팀은 기습공격을 가했다.

Japan team undertook a _______ _______.

Listen and Fill in the Blanks.

Yesterday, December 7th, 1941 — a date which will live in ______ — the United States of America was _______ and __________ attacked by naval and air forces of the Empire of Japan.

The United States was at peace with that nation and, at the ________ of Japan, was still in conversation with its government and its emperor looking toward the maintenance of peace in the Pacific.

Indeed, one hour after Japanese air squadrons had commenced bombing in the American island of Oahu, the Japanese ambassador to the United States and his colleague delivered to our Secretary of State a formal reply to a recent American message. And while this reply stated that it seemed useless to continue the existing diplomatic negotiations, it contained no threat or hint of war or of armed attack.

It will be recorded that the distance of Hawaii from Japan makes it obvious that the attack was _______ _______many days or even weeks ago. During the intervening time, the Japanese government has deliberately sought to deceive the United States by false statements and expressions of hope for continued peace.

The attack yesterday on the Hawaiian islands has ______ _____ ______ to American naval and military forces. I regret to tell you that very many American lives ______ ______ ______. In addition, American ships have been reported torpedoed on the ______ ______ between San Francisco and Honolulu.

To Develop Critical Thinking

The address by Franklin Roosevelt was made when Japan abruptly and secretly undertook a surprise attack to Pearl Harbor at Hawaii. Above all, he showed the American people his firm determination against the enemy. What do you think about Franklin Roosevelt's response as president?

A Golf Joke

Two men were golfing, and the fairway of the hole they were playing was adjacent to a road. The first man was setting up for his swing, when a funeral procession went by on the road. He stopped, faced the procession for a moment, then bowed his head in prayer as the hearse passed by. Only when the procession had passed out of view did he resume playing, driving his ball to the green. As they were walking toward the green, the second man said, "That was a touching show of respect for the deceased back there. I had no idea you were so sentimental." The first man shrugged and said, "It's the least I could do. I was married to her for thirty years."

www.jokesaboutamericans.com/

Whole Language Approach
Internet-Aided English Learning 1

SELECTED TOP

Epoch-Making Speeches

Published February 2012
First Published February 2010
SHINASA Publishing Co.
28-36 NokBeon-Dong, EunPyung-Gu, Seoul, Korea
Registered : 9-52 (Jan. 5 1956)
Tel : 02-382-6411
Fax : 02-382-6401
E-mail : shinasa@chol.com / Homepage : www.shinasa.co.kr
ISBN : 978-89-8396-670-4
Printed and bounded in Korea

₩ 10,000